FOR ORGANS, PIANOS & ELECTRONIC KEYBOARDS

E-Z PLAY® TODAY

339

20th ANNIVERSARY
John TRAVOLTA Olivia

GREASE

is *still* the word

T0040621

CONTENTS

PARAMOUNT PICTURES PRESENTS A ROBERT STIGWOOD/ALLAN CARR PRODUCTION JOHN TRAVOLTA OLIVIA NEWTON-JOHN "GREASE" AND STOCKARD CHANNING AS RIZZO WITH SPECIAL GUEST APPEARANCES BY EVE ARDEN, FRANKIE AVALON, JOAN BLONDELL, EDD BYRNES, SID CAESAR, ALICE GHOSTLEY, DODY GOODMAN, SHA-NA-NA SCREENPLAY BY BRONTE WOODARD ADAPTATION BY ALLAN CARR BASED ON THE ORIGINAL MUSICAL BY JIM JACOBS AND WARREN CASEY PRODUCED ON THE BROADWAY STAGE BY KENNETH WAISSMAN AND MAXINE FOX IN ASSOCIATION WITH ANTHONY D'AMATO CHOREOGRAPHY BY PATRICIA BIRCH

PG PARENTAL GUIDANCE SUGGESTED
SOME MATERIAL MAY NOT BE SUITABLE FOR CHILDREN
DIGITAL dts SOUND
DOLBY DIGITAL
SOUNDTRACK ON POLYDOR CDs AND CASSETTES www.greasemovie.com
PRODUCED BY ROBERT STIGWOOD AND ALLAN CARR DIRECTED BY RANDAL KLEISER
TM & COPYRIGHT © 1998 BY PARAMOUNT PICTURES ALL RIGHTS RESERVED.
A VIACOM COMPANY

ISBN 978-0-634-00298-4

**HAL•LEONARD®
CORPORATION**
7777 W. BLUEMOUND RD. P.O. BOX 13819 MILWAUKEE, WI 53213

Visit Hal Leonard Online at
www.halleonard.com

Grease

Registration 4
Rhythm: Rock or Pops

Words and Music by
Barry Gibb

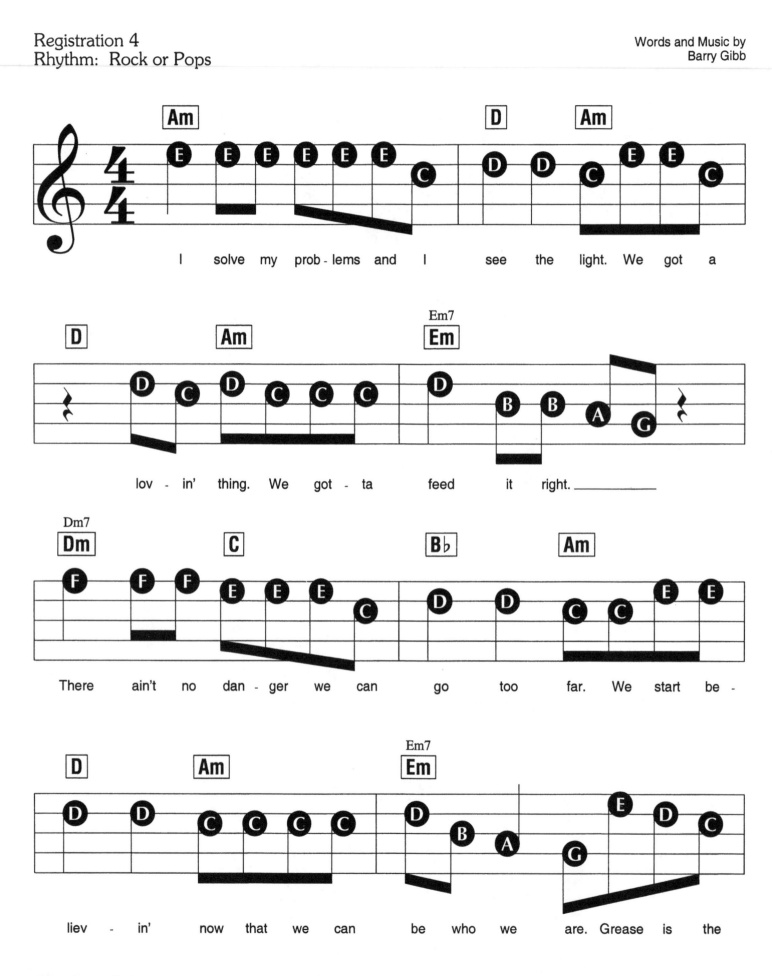

I solve my prob-lems and I see the light. We got a lov-in' thing. We got-ta feed it right. There ain't no dan-ger we can go too far. We start be-liev-in' now that we can be who we are. Grease is the

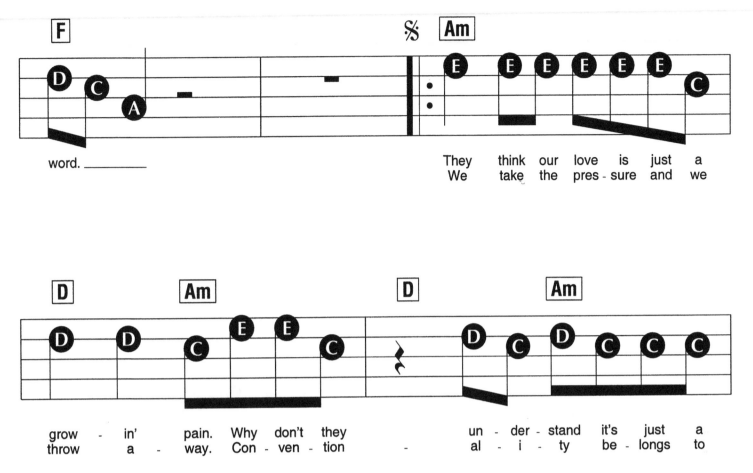

word. _____

They think our love is just a
We take the pres - sure and we

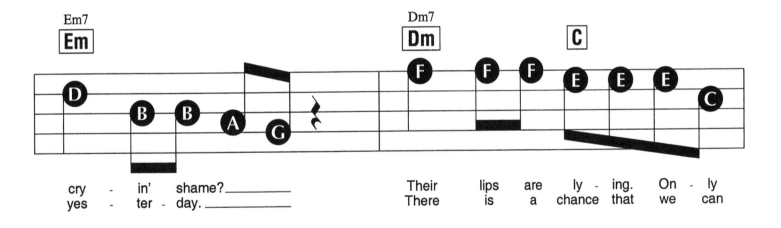

grow - in' pain. Why don't they
throw a - way. Con - ven - tion

un - der - stand it's just a
al - i - ty be - longs to

cry - in' shame? _____
yes - ter - day. _____

Their lips are ly - ing. On - ly
There is a chance that we can

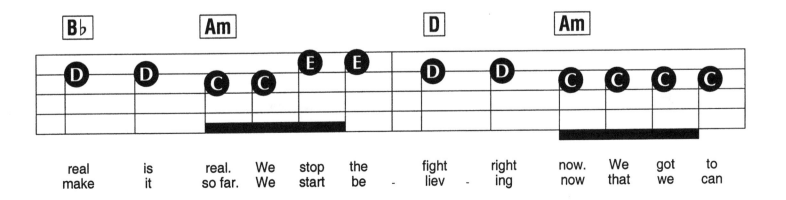

real is real. We stop the
make it so far. We start

fight right now. We got to
be - liev - ing now now that we can

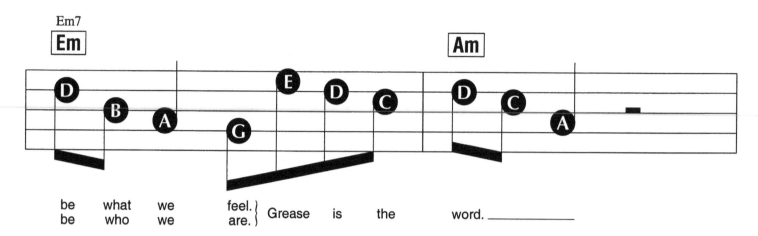

be what we feel.
be who we are. Grease is the word. _____

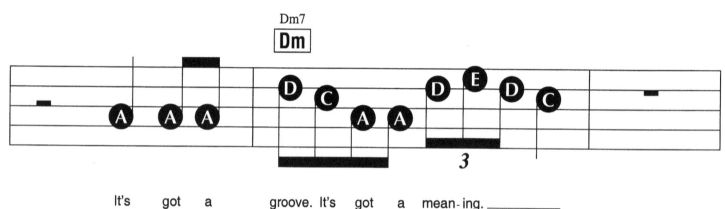

It's got a groove. It's got a mean - ing. _____

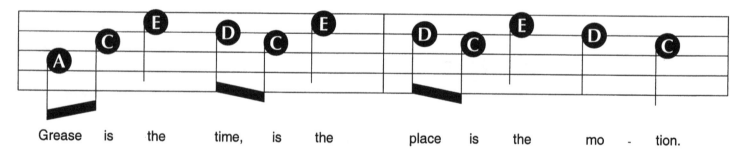

Grease is the time, is the place is the mo - tion.

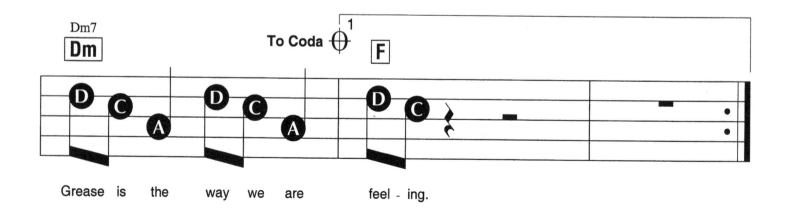

Grease is the way we are feel - ing.

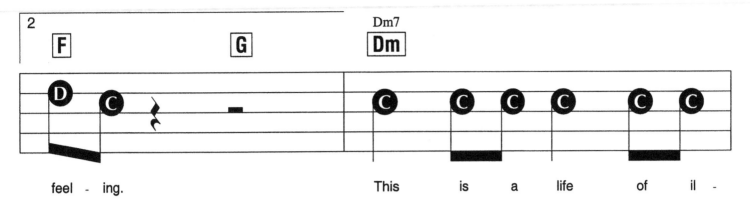

feel - ing.　　　　This　is　a　life　of　il -

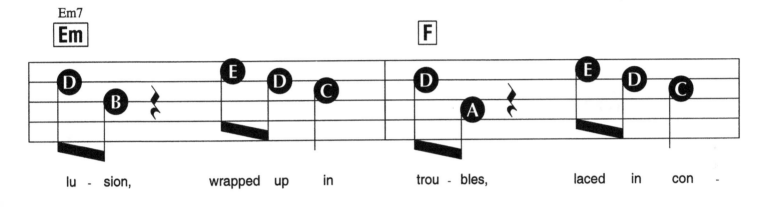

lu - sion,　　wrapped　up　in　trou - bles,　　laced　in　con -

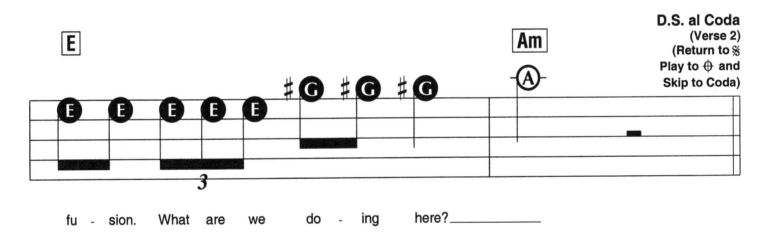

D.S. al Coda
(Verse 2)
(Return to 𝄋
Play to ⊕ and
Skip to Coda)

fu - sion. What　are　we　do - ing　here?＿＿＿＿＿

CODA

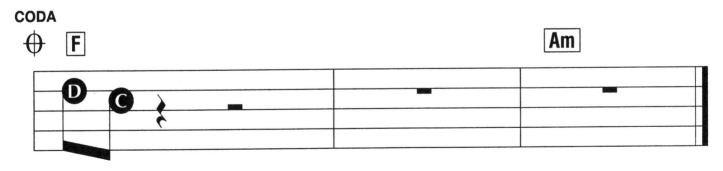

feel - ing.

Hopelessly Devoted to You

Registration 10
Rhythm: Waltz

Words and Music by
John Farrar

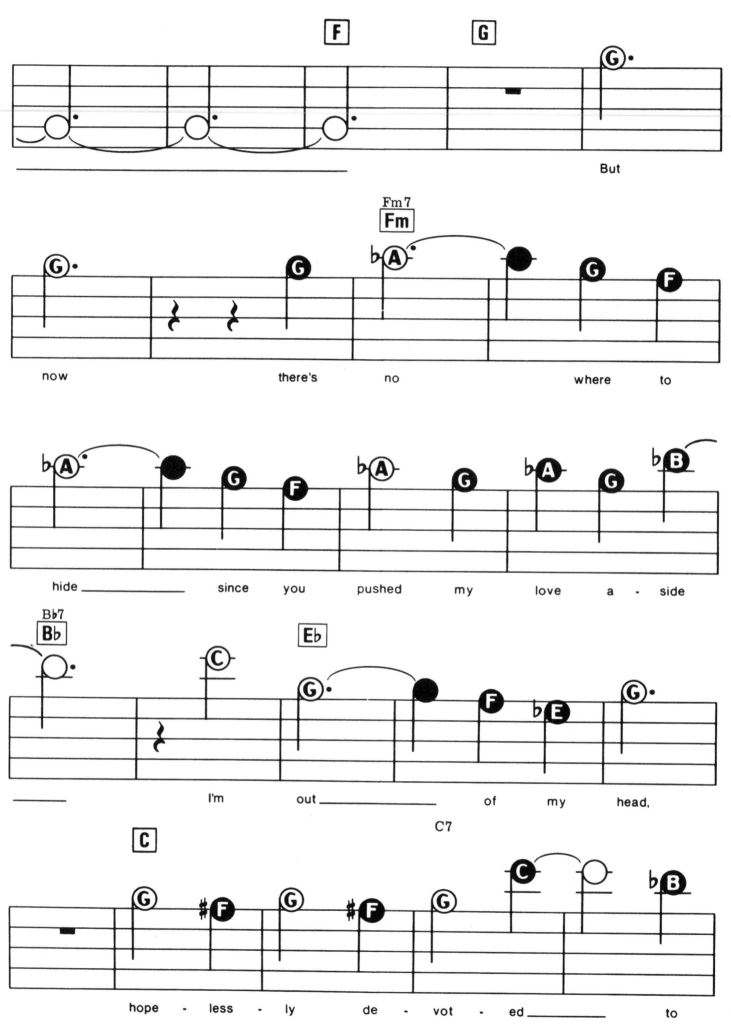

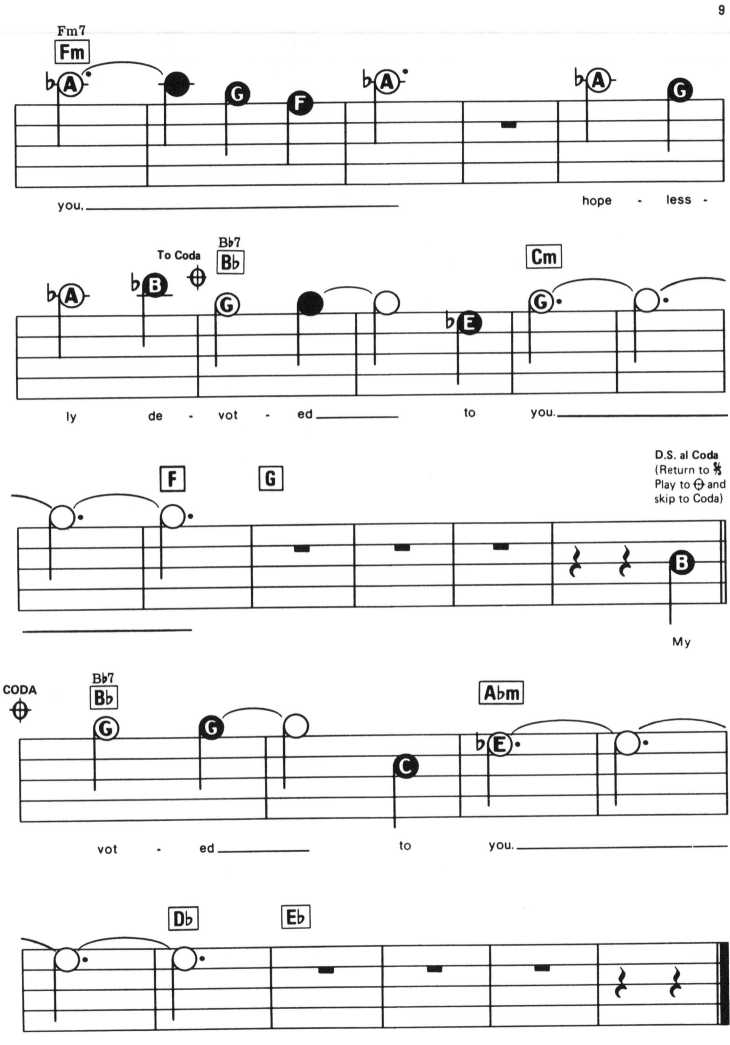

You're the One That I Want

Registration 4
Rhythm: Rock or 8 Beat

Words and Music by
John Farrar

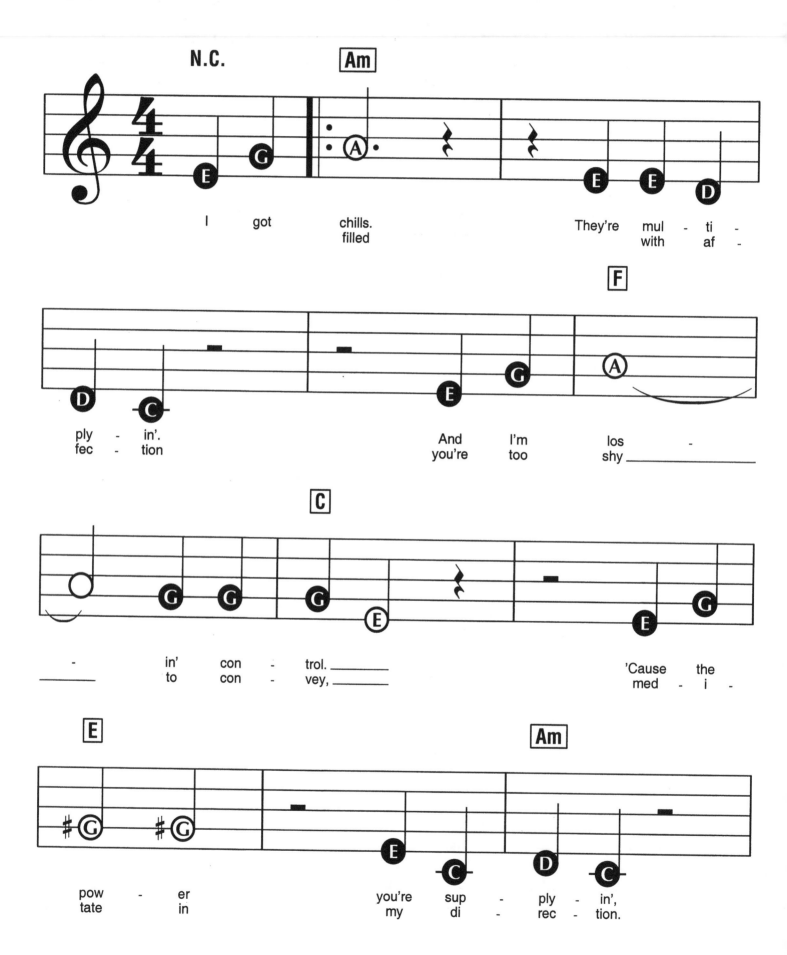

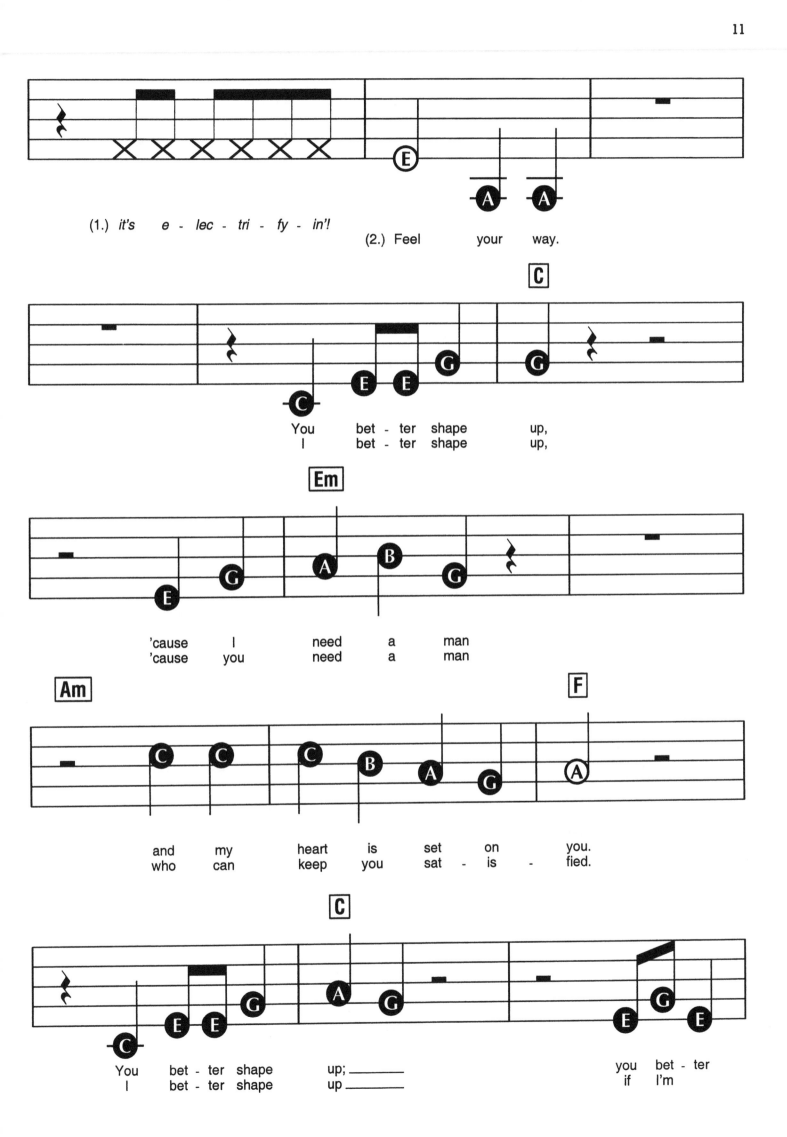

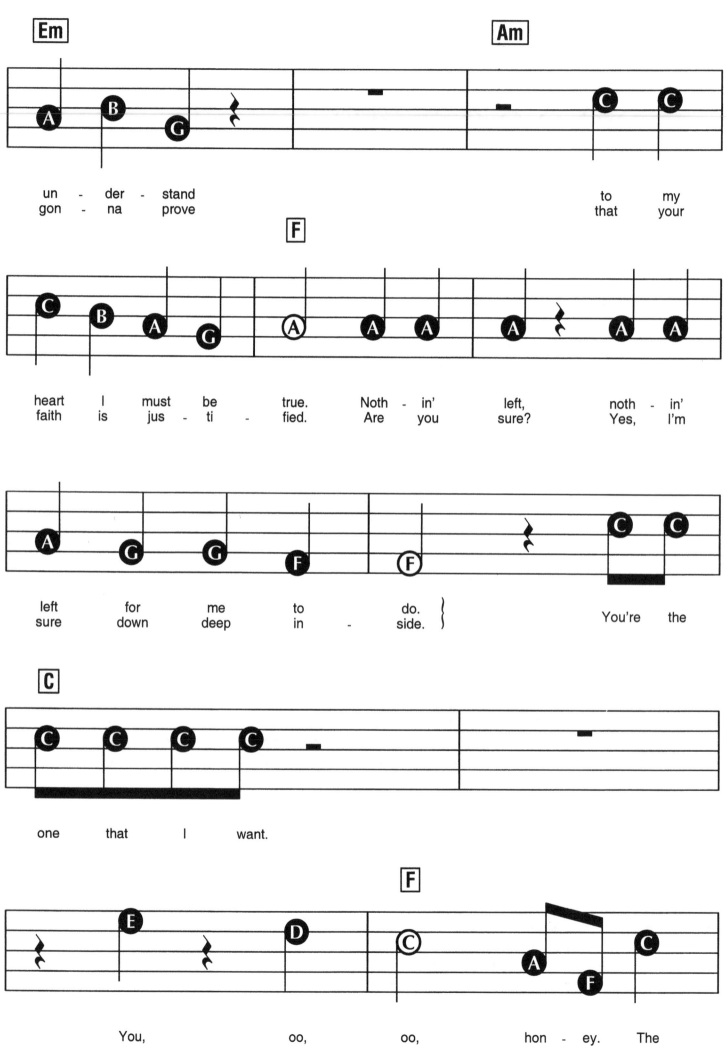

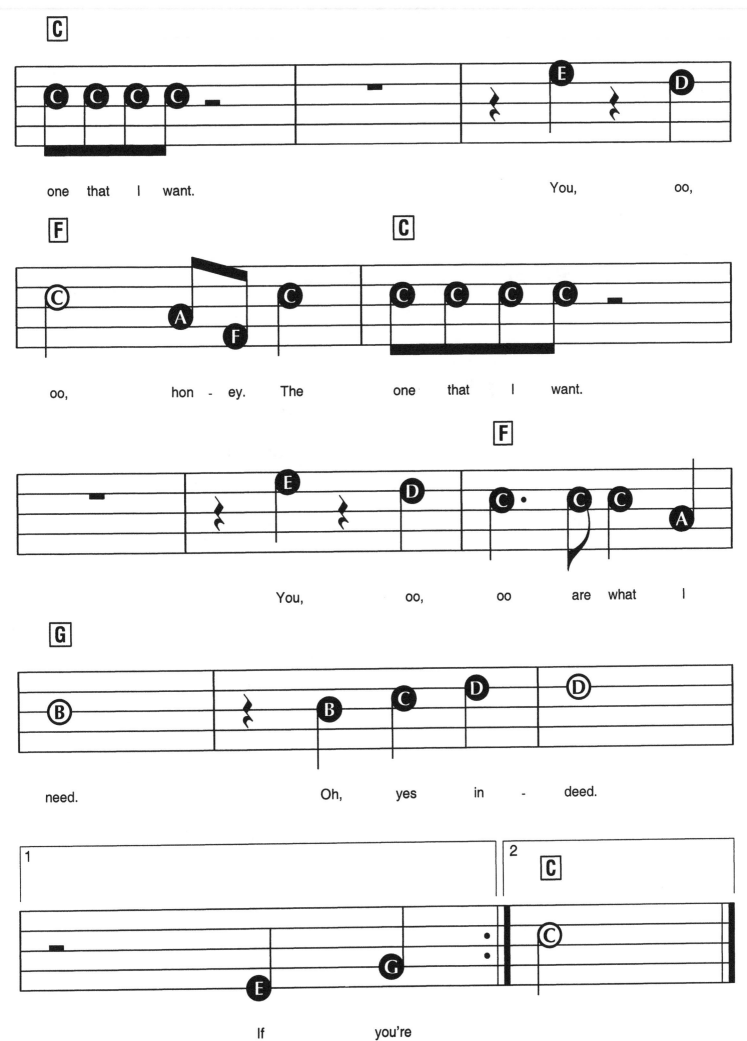

Sandy

Registration 8
Rhythm: None

Words and Music by Scott Simon
and Louis St. Louis

Rhythm: Rock or Pops

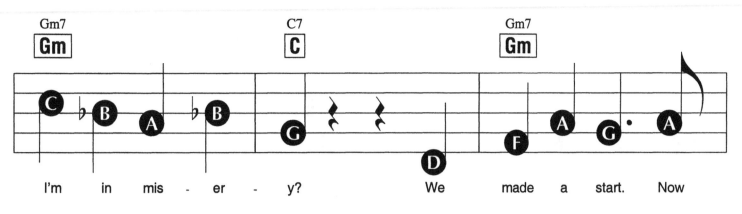

I'm in mis - er - y? We made a start. Now

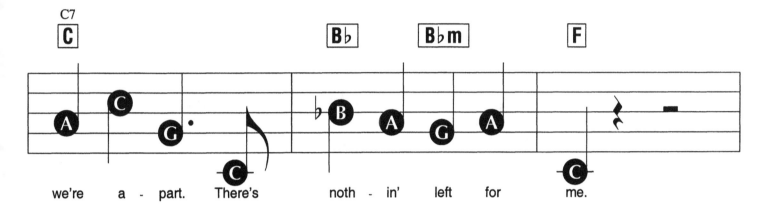

we're a - part. There's noth - in' left for me.

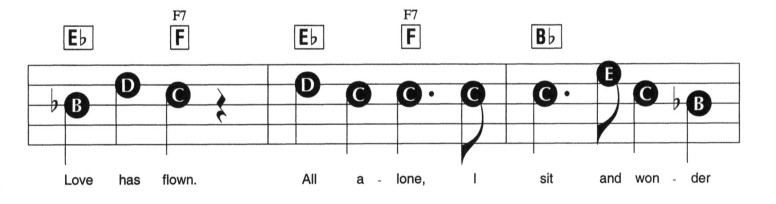

Love has flown. All a - lone, I sit and won - der

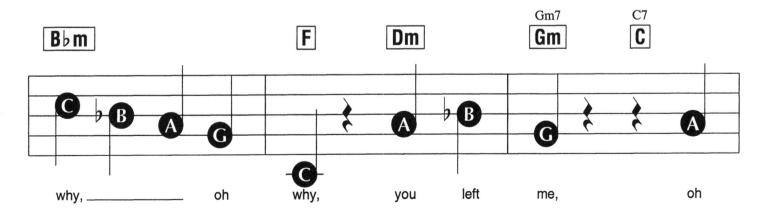

why, _____ oh why, you left me, oh

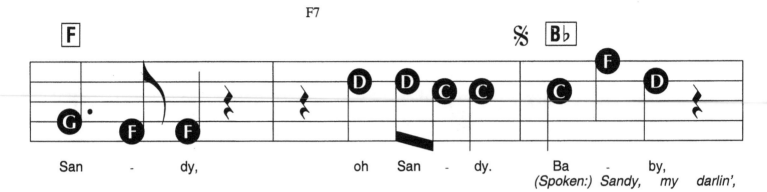

San - dy, oh San - dy. Ba - by,
(Spoken:) Sandy, my darlin',

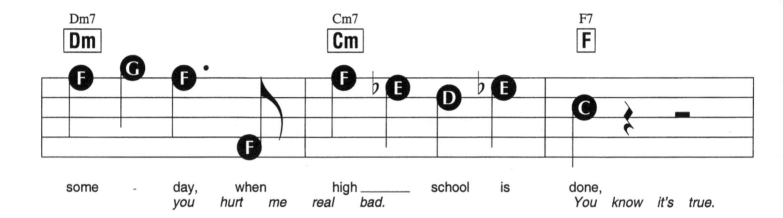

some - day, when high _____ school is done,
you hurt me real bad. *You know it's true.*

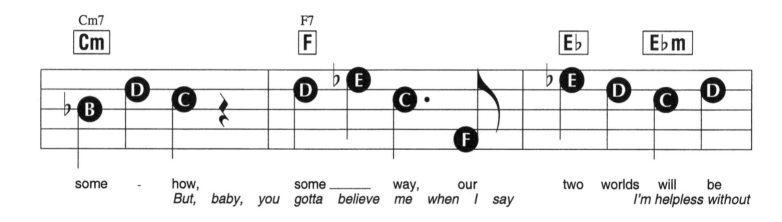

some - how, some _____ way, our two worlds will be
But, baby, you gotta believe me when I say *I'm helpless without*

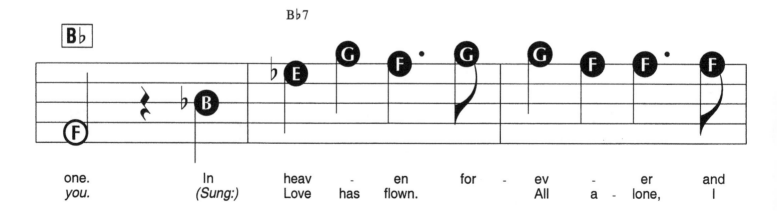

one. In heav - en for - ev - er and
you. *(Sung:) Love has flown.* *All a - lone, I*

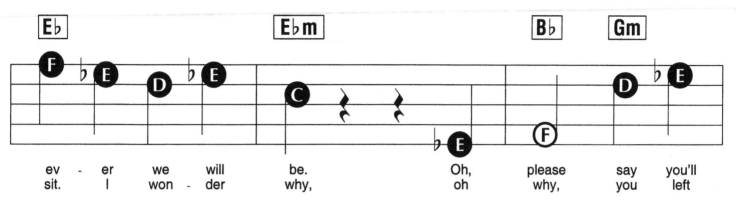

ev - er we will be. Oh, please say you'll
sit. I won - der why, oh why, say you left

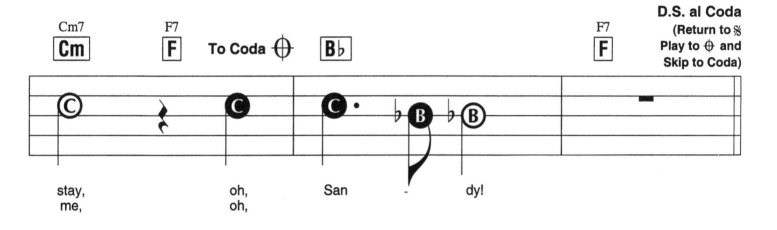

stay, oh, San - dy!
me, oh,

D.S. al Coda
(Return to %
Play to ⊕ and
Skip to Coda)

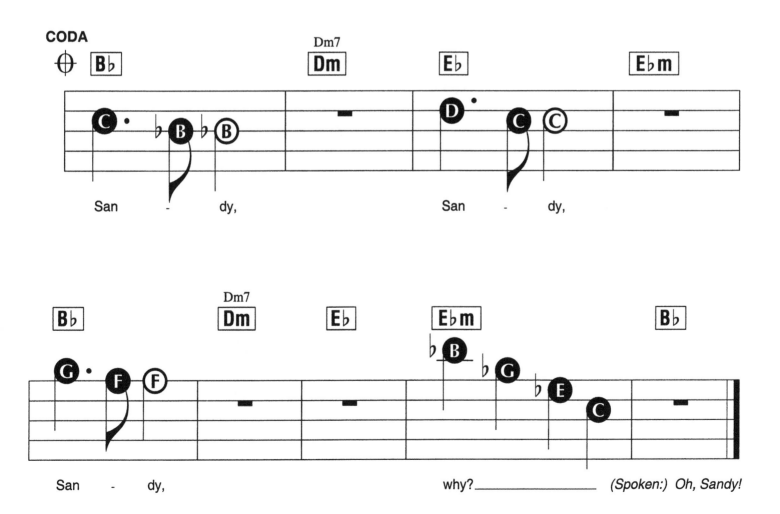

CODA

San - dy, San - dy,

San - dy, why?_____ *(Spoken:) Oh, Sandy!*

Beauty School Dropout

Registration 2
Rhythm: None

Lyric and Music by Warren Casey
and Jim Jacobs

N.C. | Eb | Cm7 Cm | Fm7 Fm | Bb

Your sto - ry's sad to tell: a teen-age ne'er-do-well; most

Gm7 Gm | Cm7 Cm | Fm7 Fm | Bb

mixed - up non - de - lin - quent on the block. Your

Gm7 Gm | C7 C | Fm7 Fm | Db7 Db

fu - ture's so un - clear now. What's left of your ca - reer now? Can't

Eb | Cm7 Cm | Rhythm: Waltz Abm

e - ven get a trade - in on your smock.

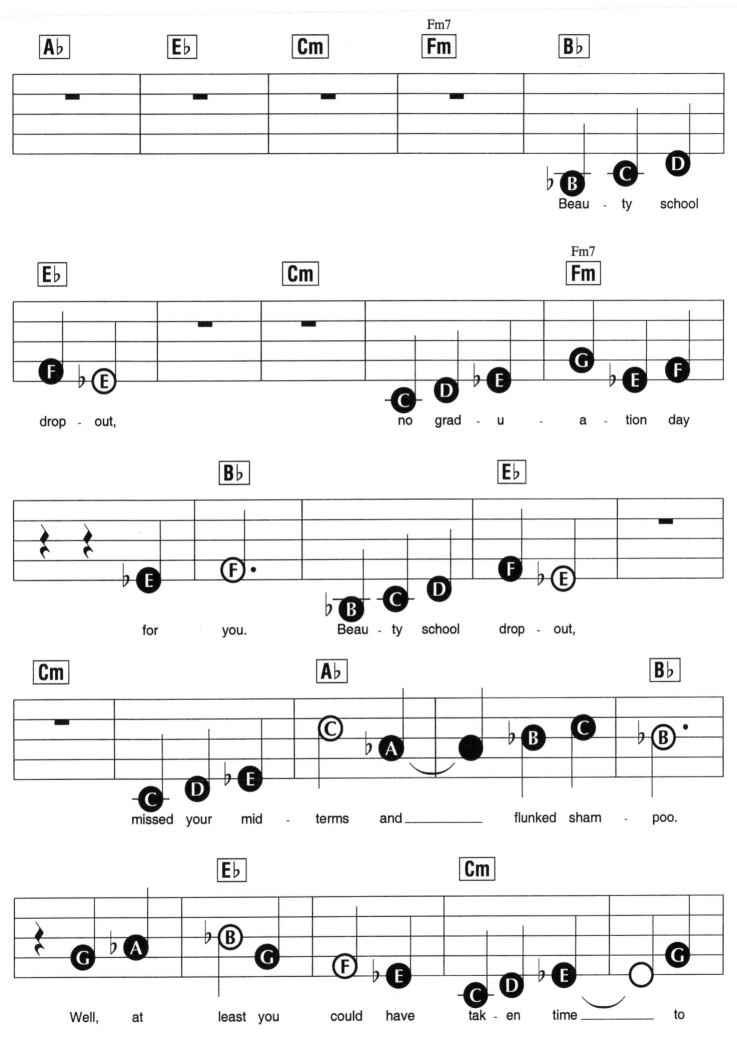

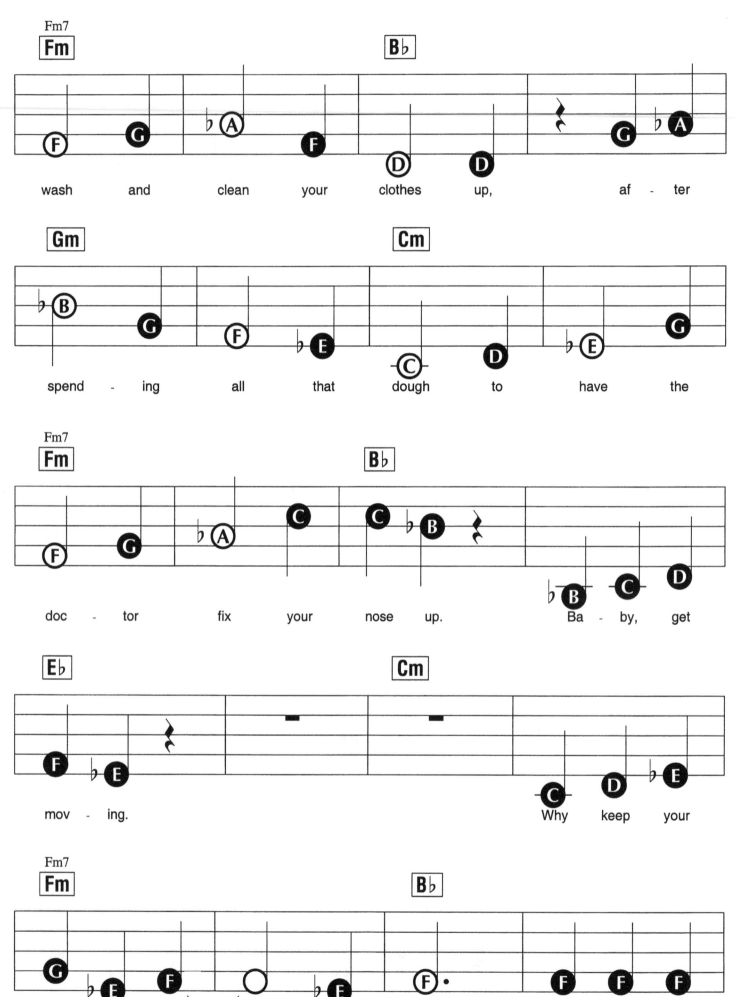

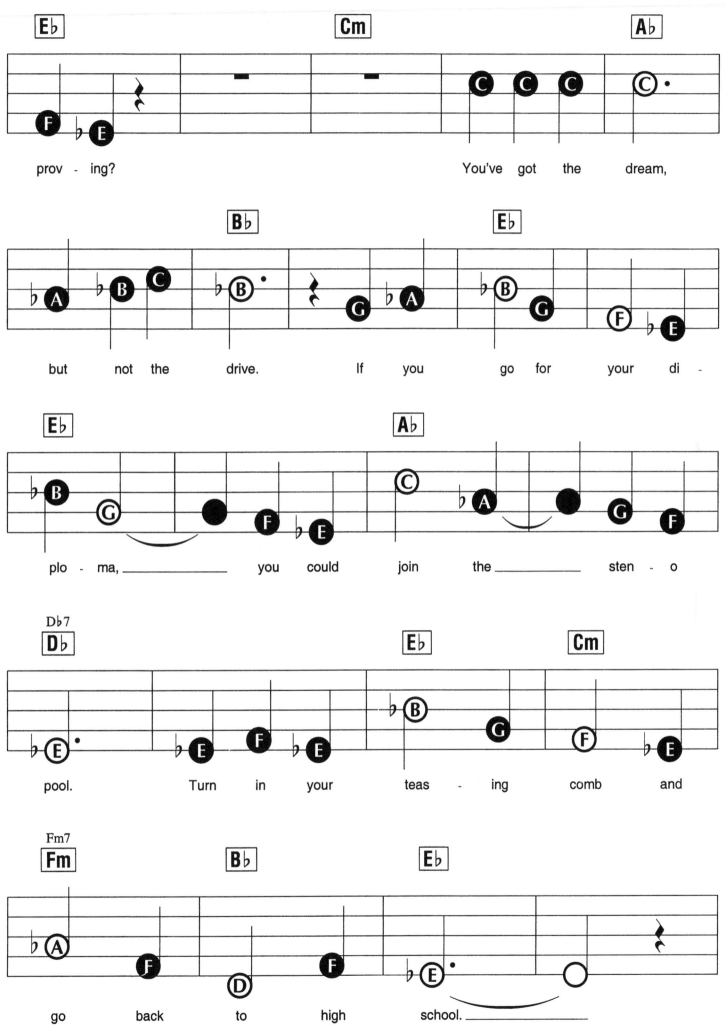

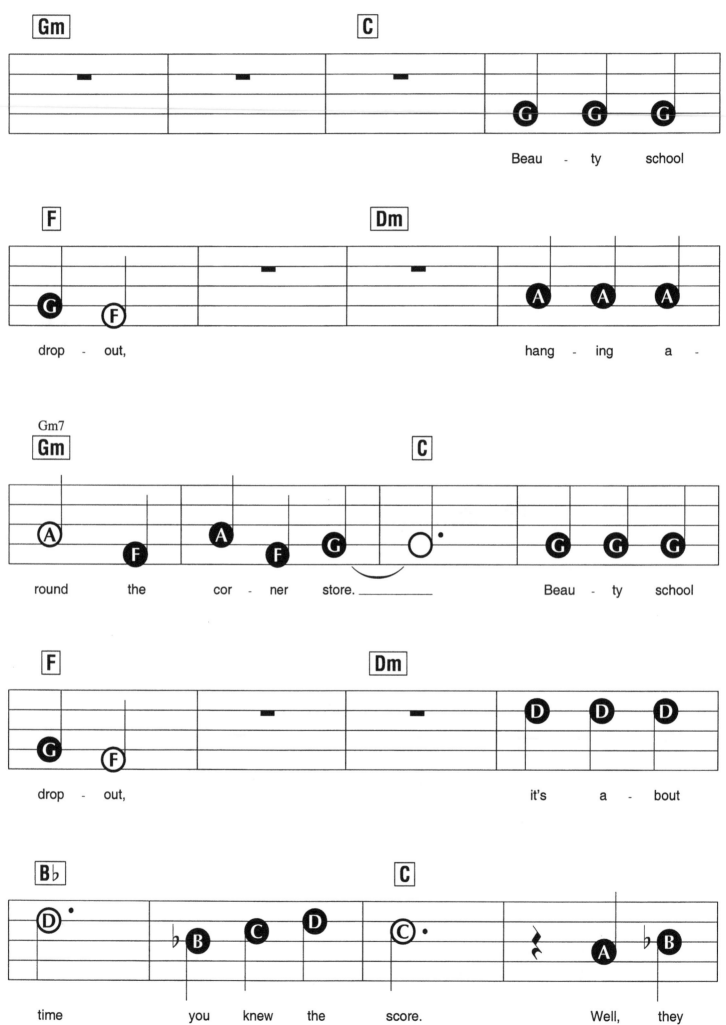

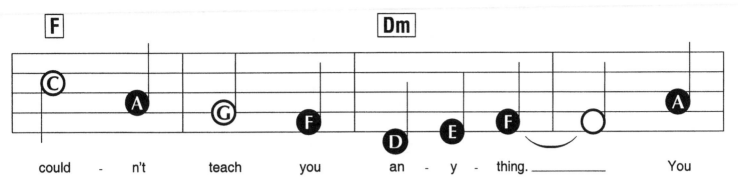

could - n't   teach   you   an - y - thing. _____ You

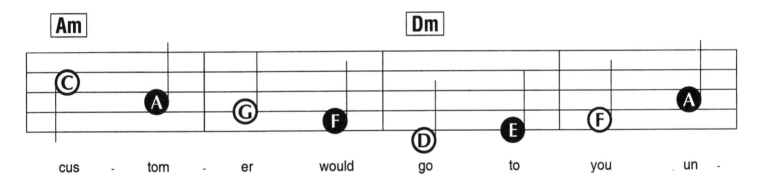

think   you're   such   a   look - er.   But   no

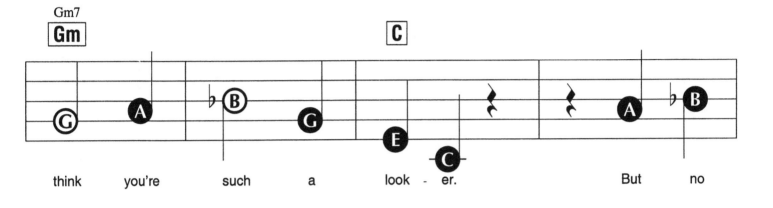

cus - tom - er   would   go   to   you   un -

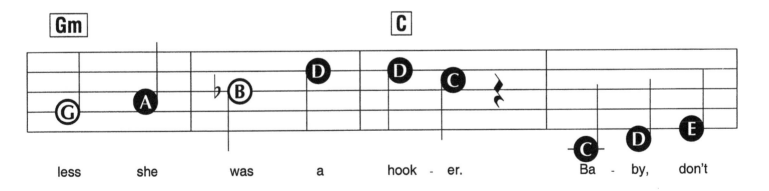

less   she   was   a   hook - er.   Ba - by,   don't

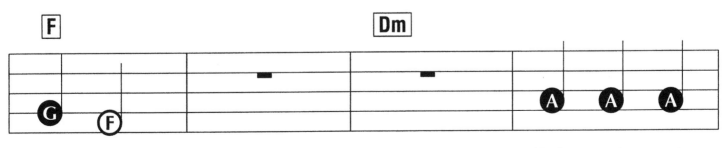

sweat   it.   You're   not   cut

24

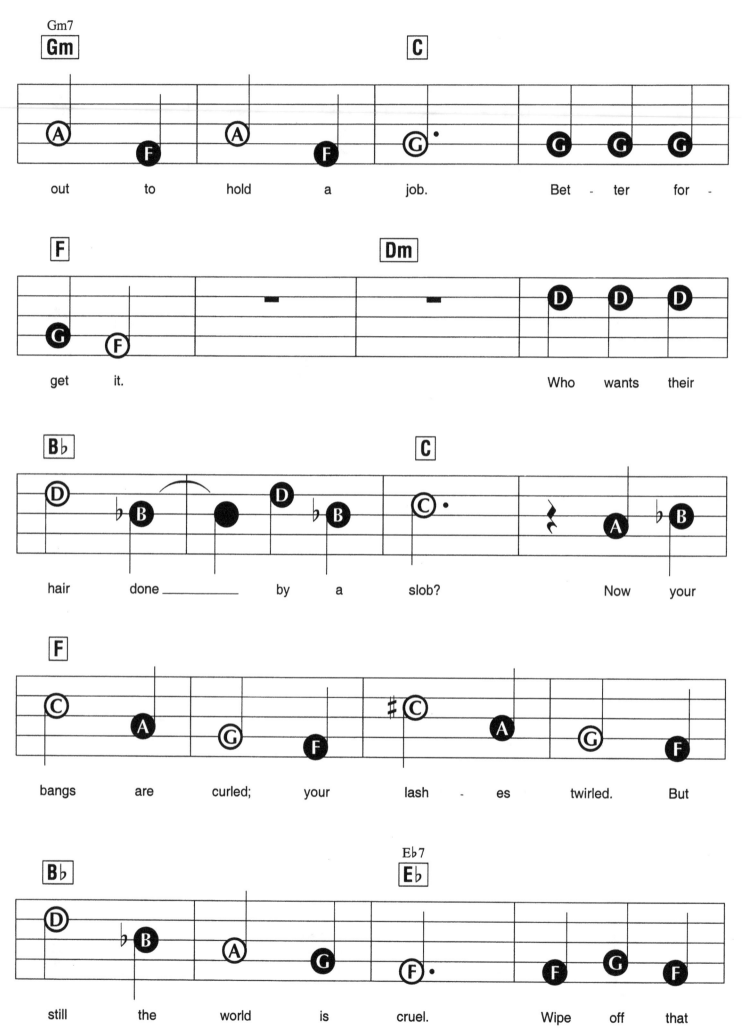

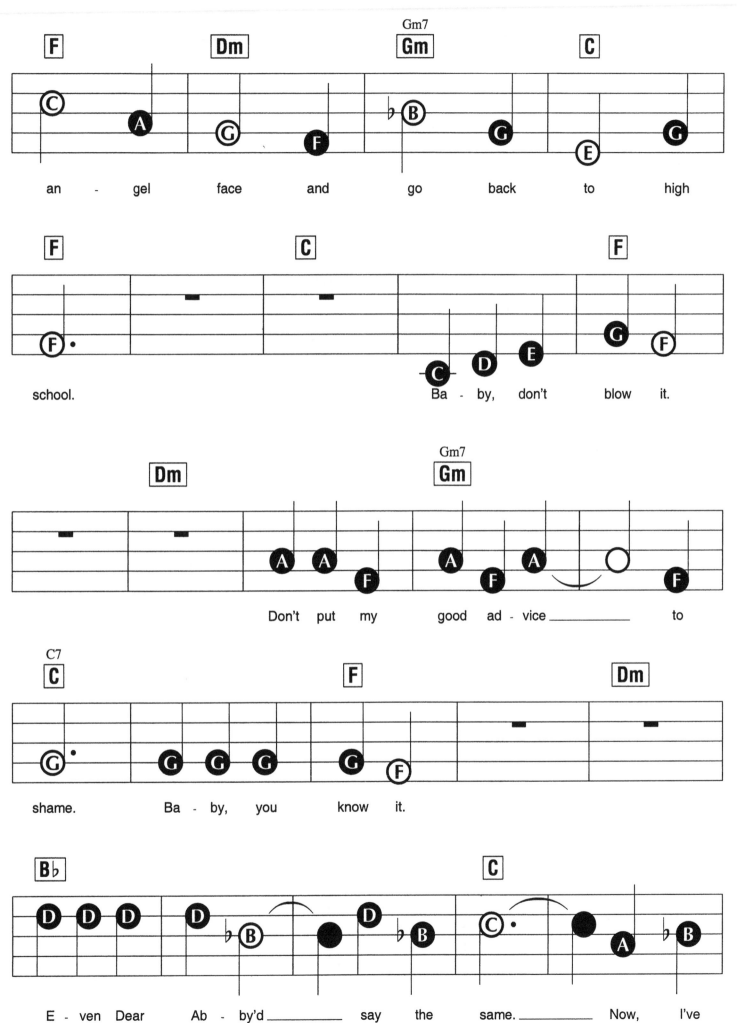

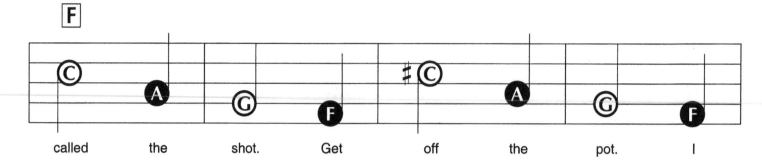

called   the   shot.   Get   off   the   pot.   I

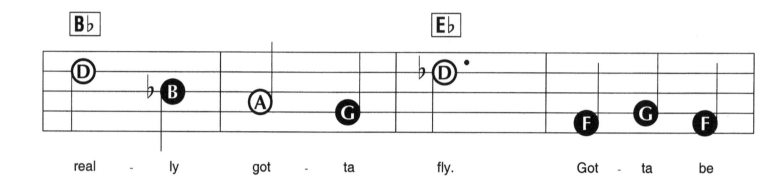

real - ly   got - ta   fly.   Got - ta   be

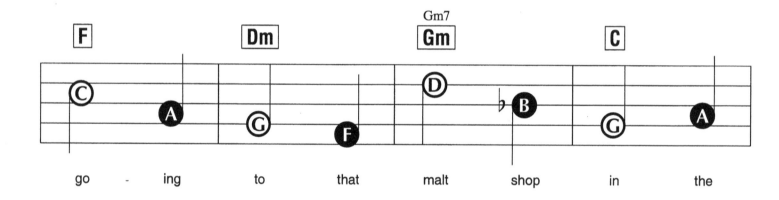

go - ing   to   that   malt   shop   in   the

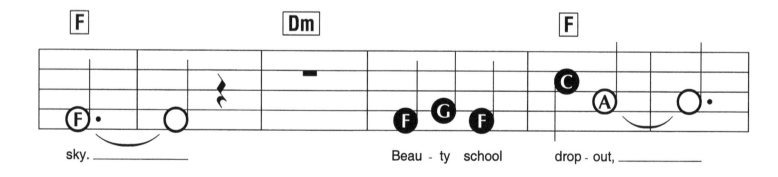

sky. _____   Beau - ty   school   drop - out, _____

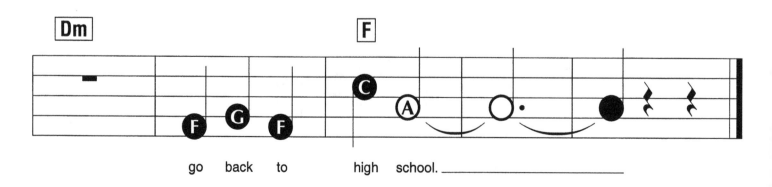

go   back   to   high   school. _____

Look at Me, I'm Sandra Dee

Registration 10
Rhythm: Waltz

Lyric and Music by Warren Casey
and Jim Jacobs

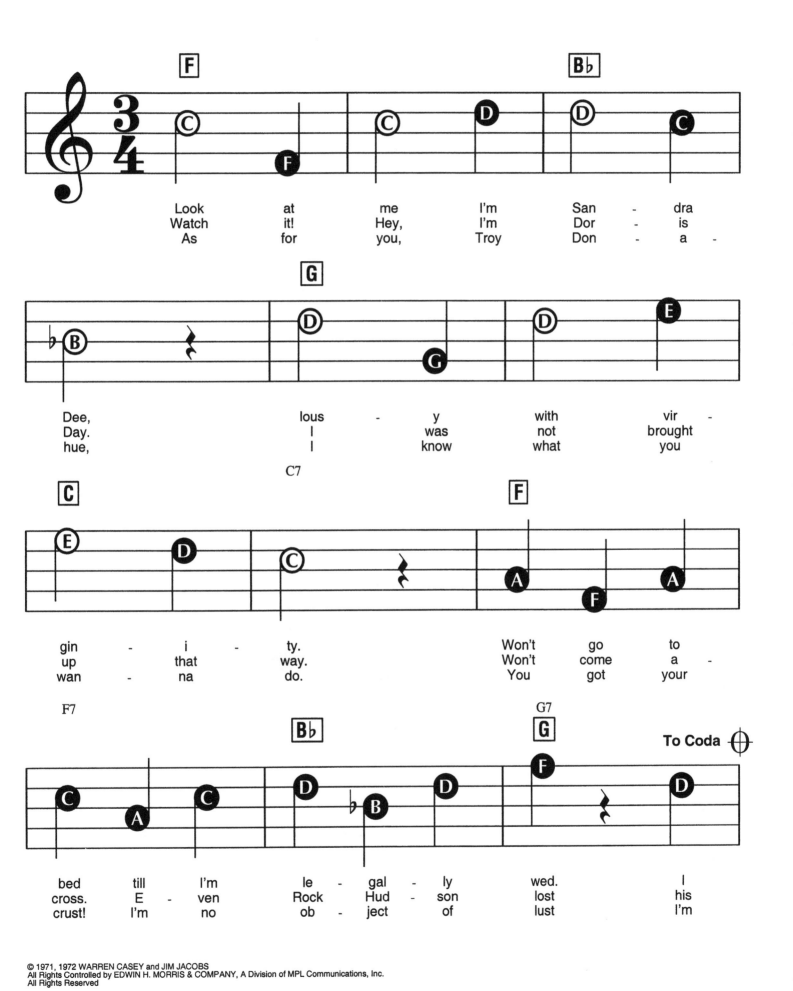

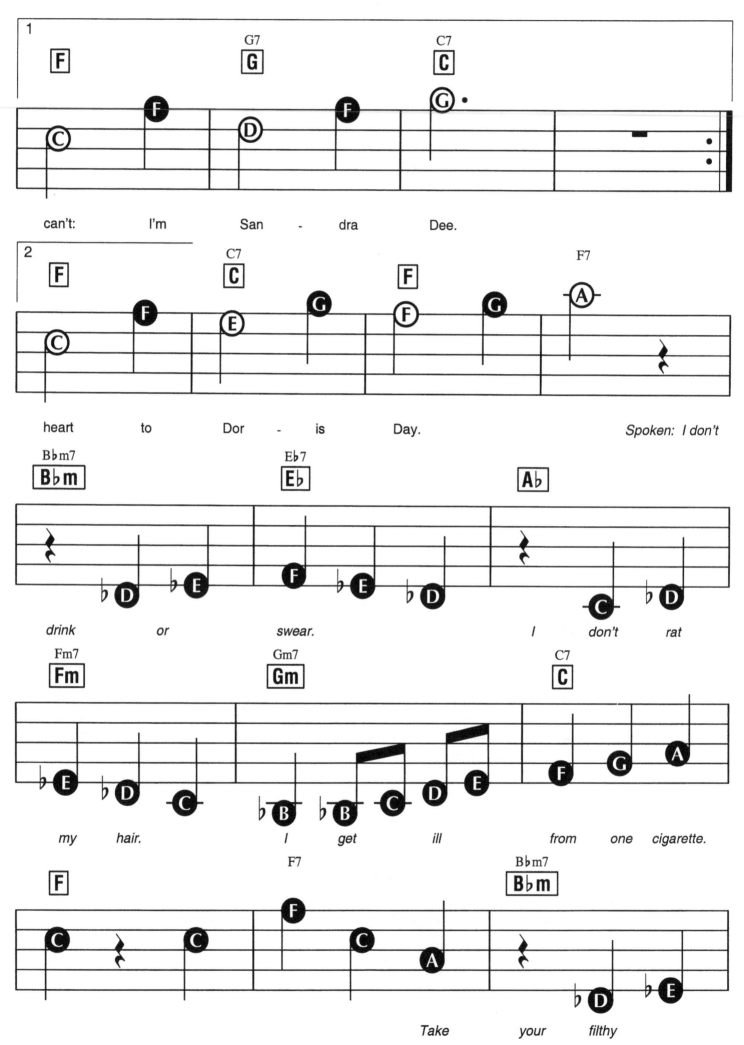

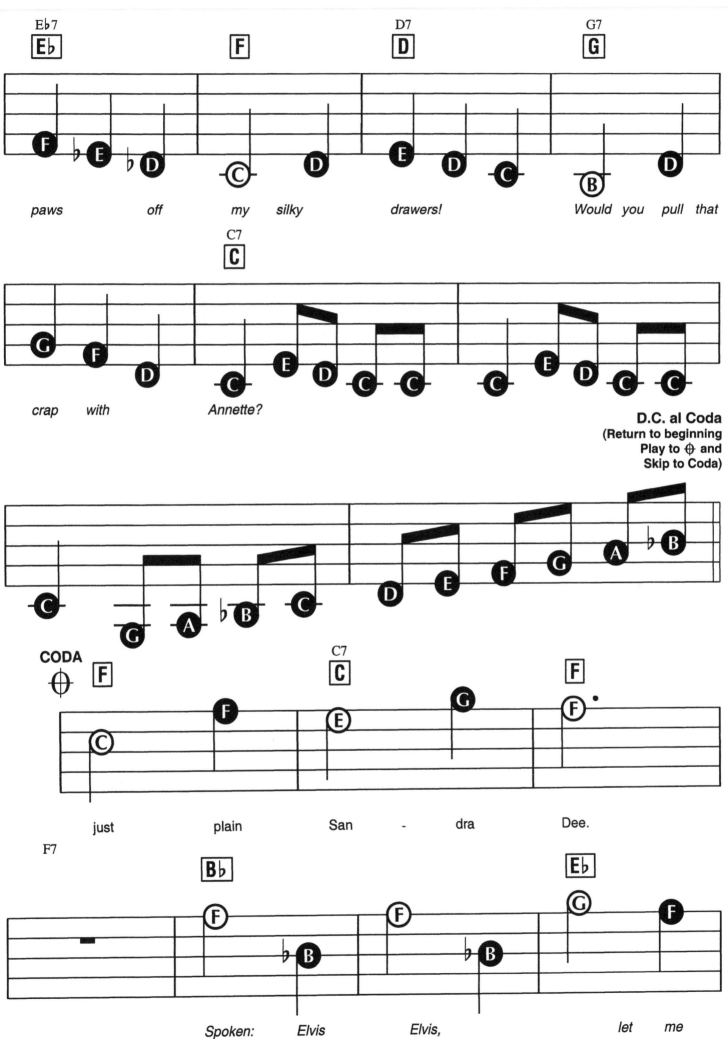

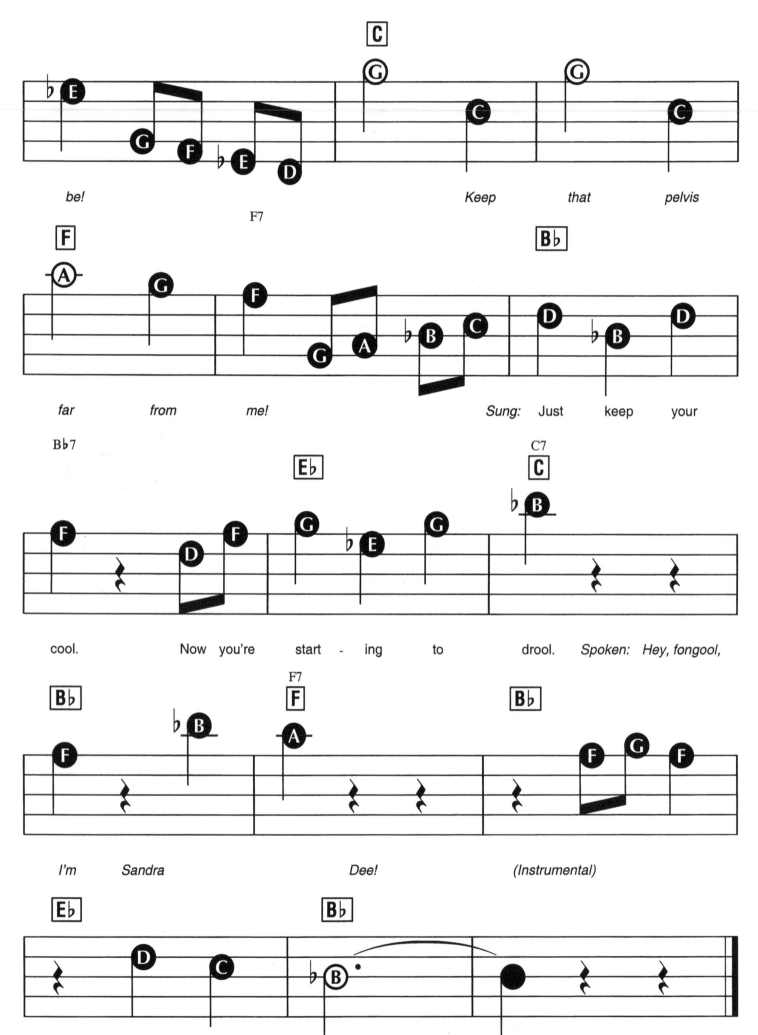

Summer Nights

Registration 2
Rhythm: Swing or Fox Trot

Lyric and Music by Warren Casey
and Jim Jacobs

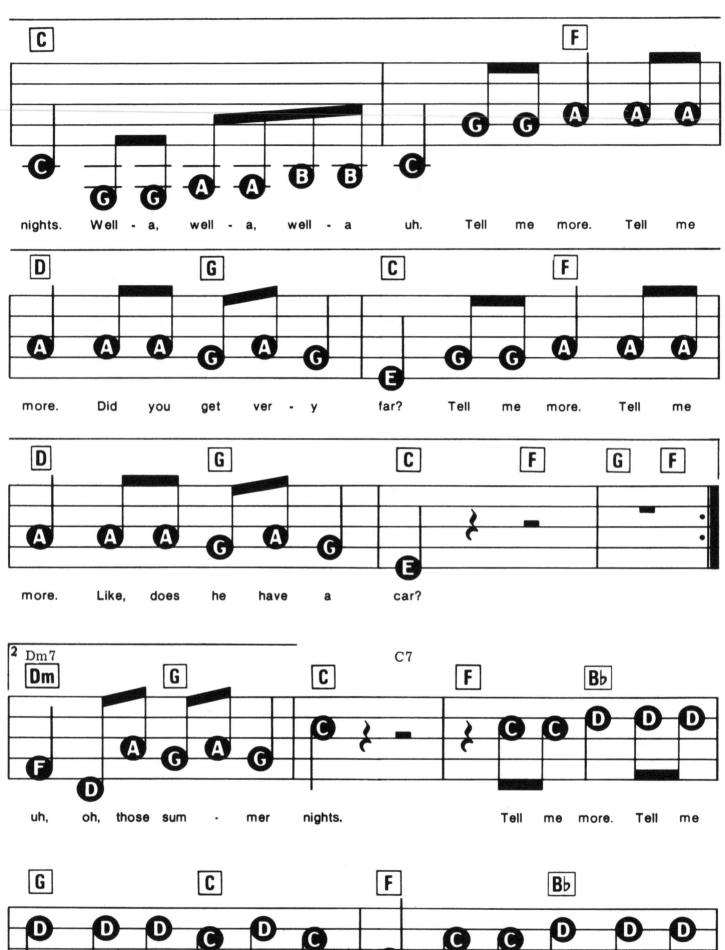

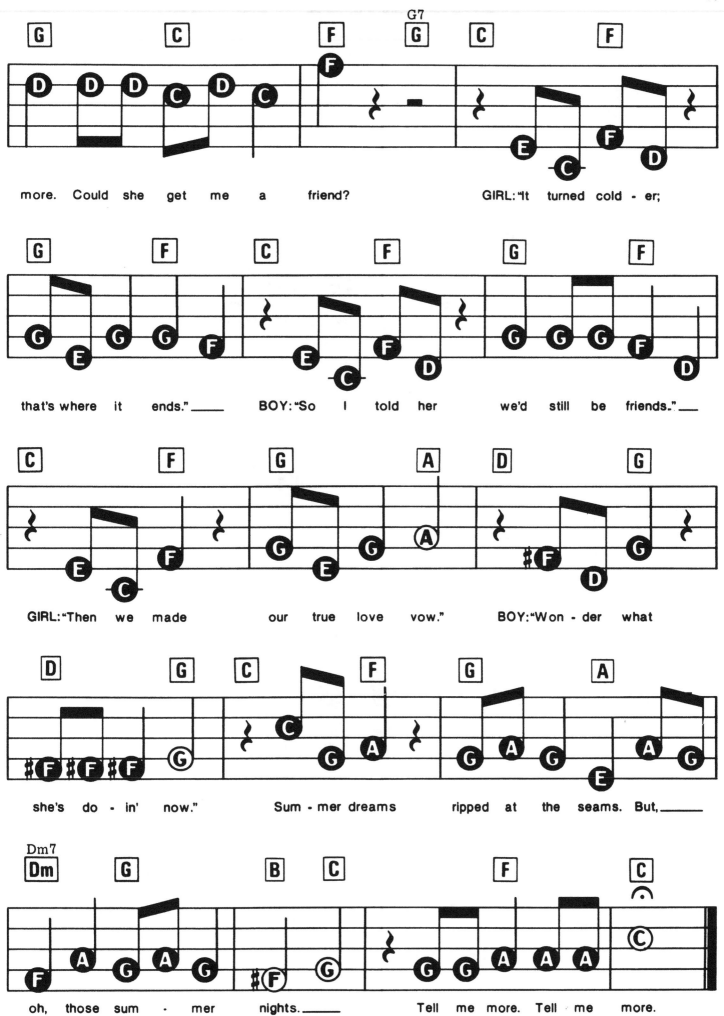

Greased Lightnin'

Registration 9
Rhythm: Rock or Pops

Lyric and Music by Warren Casey
and Jim Jacobs

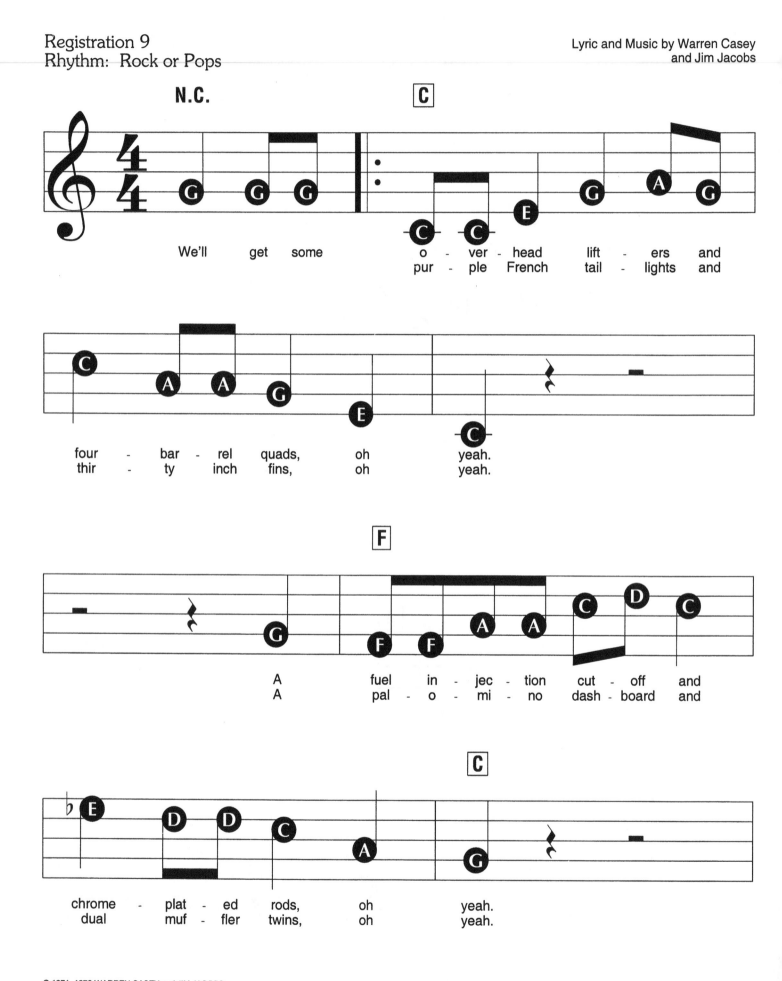

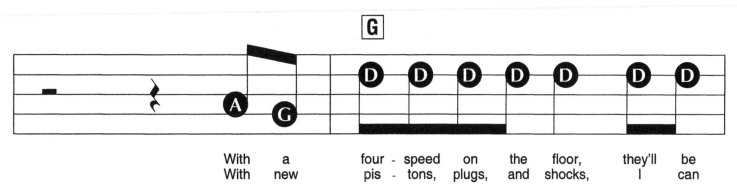

With a four - speed on the floor, they'll be
With new pis - tons, plugs, and shocks, I can

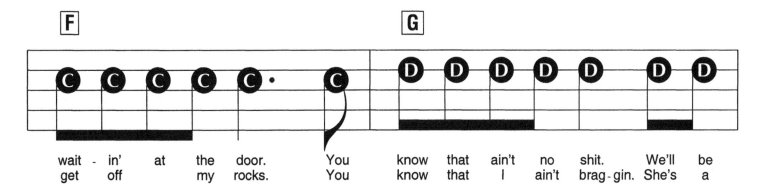

wait - in' at the door. You know that ain't no shit. We'll be
get off my rocks. You know that I ain't brag - gin. She's a

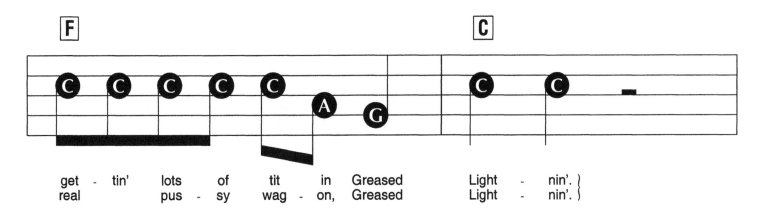

get - tin' lots of tit in Greased Light - nin'. }
real pus - sy wag - on, Greased Light - nin'. }

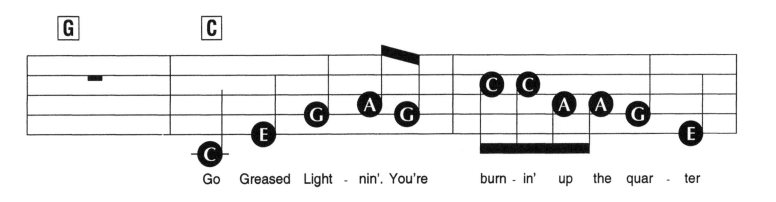

Go Greased Light - nin'. You're burn - in' up the quar - ter

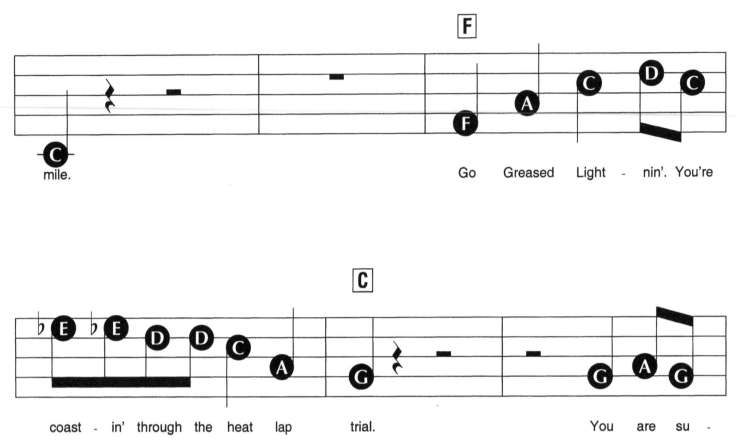

mile.　　　　　　　　　Go　Greased　Light - nin'.　You're

coast - in'　through　the　heat　lap　trial.　　　　　You　are　su -

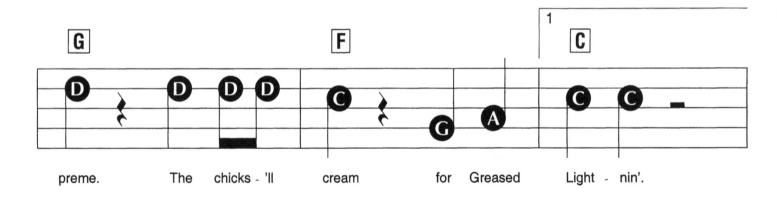

preme.　　The　chicks - 'll　cream　　for　Greased　Light - nin'.

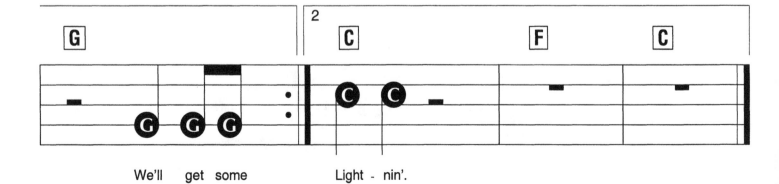

We'll　get　some　Light - nin'.

It's Raining on Prom Night

Registration 7
Rhythm: None

Lyric and Music by Warren Casey
and Jim Jacobs

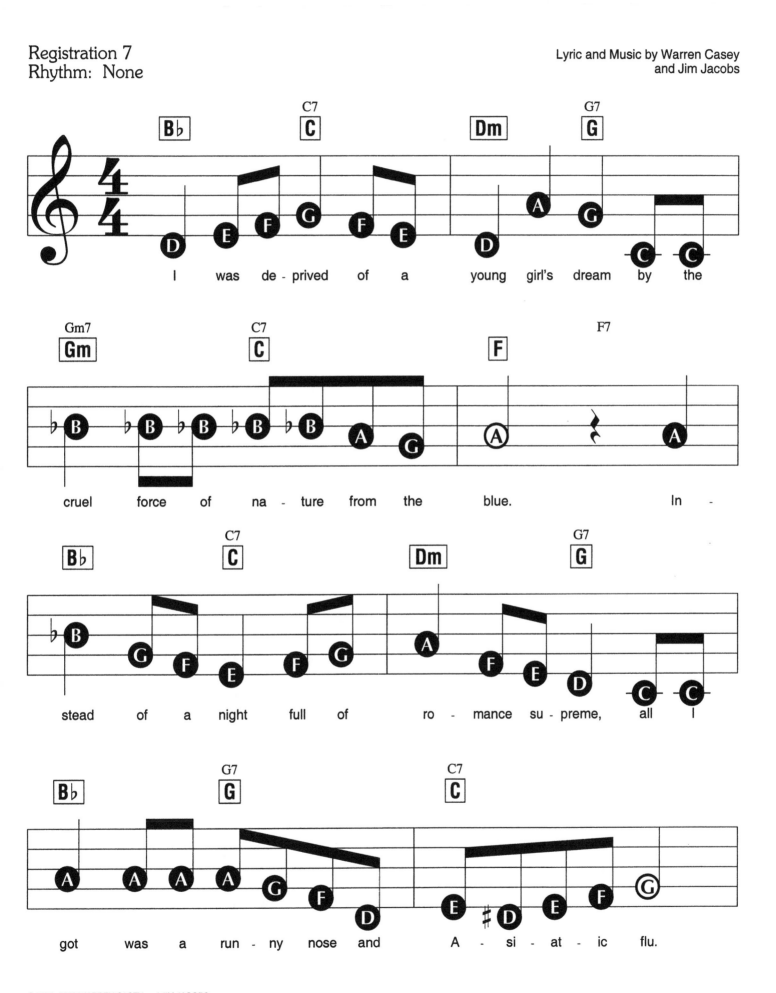

38

Rhythm: Cha-Cha or Latin

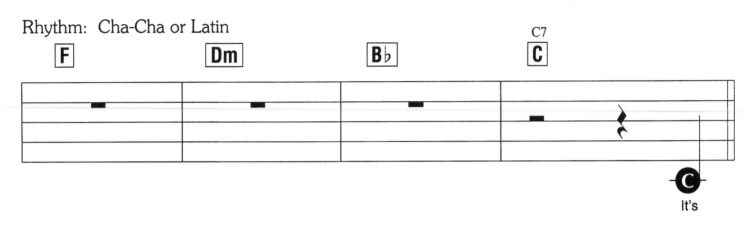

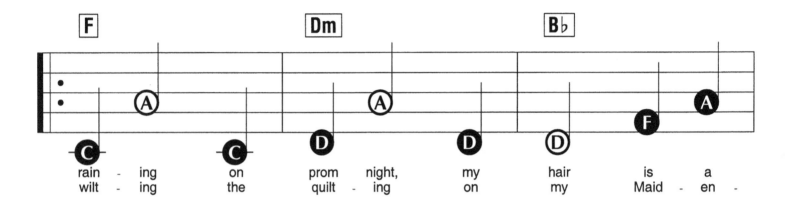

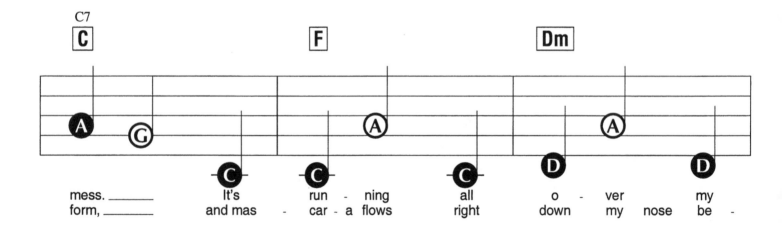

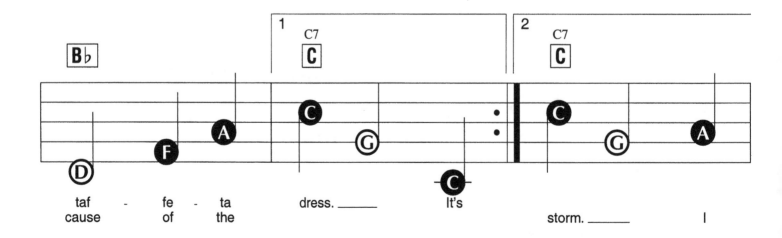

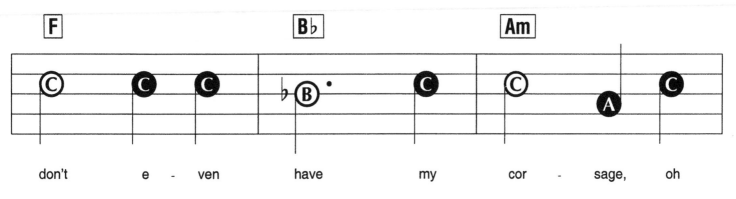

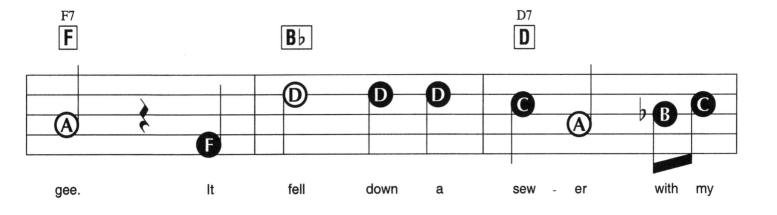

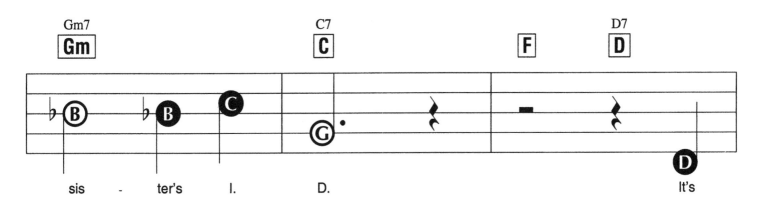

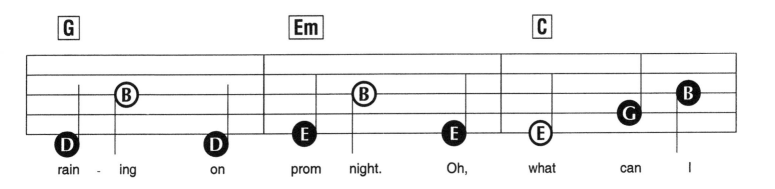

40

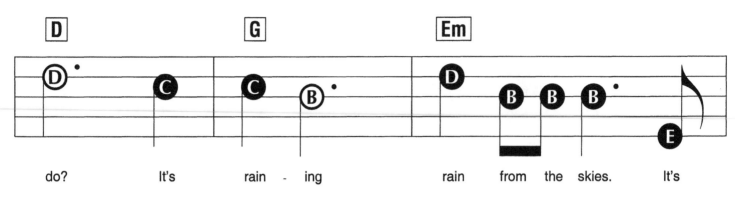

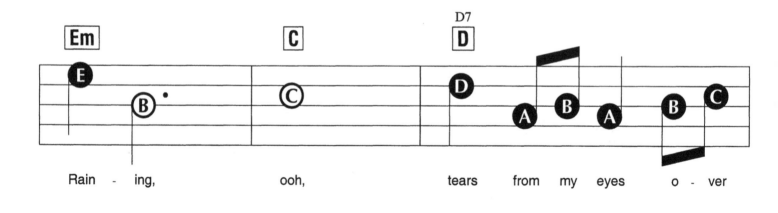

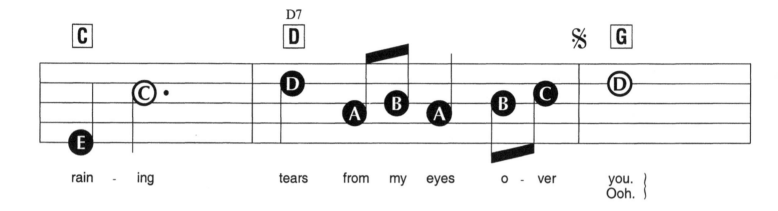

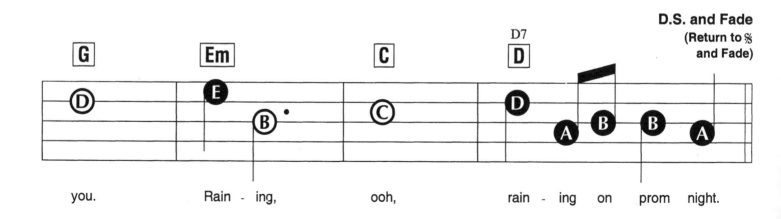

Blue Moon

Registration 8
Rhythm: Swing

Words by Lorenz Hart
Music by Richard Rodgers

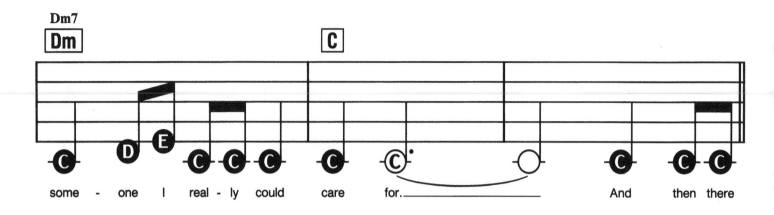

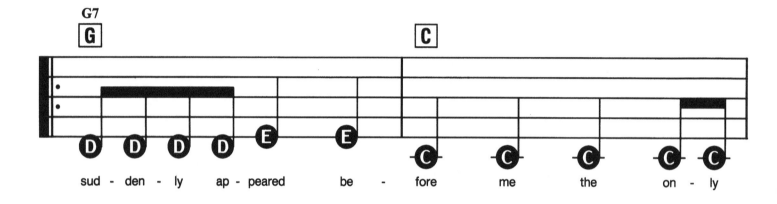

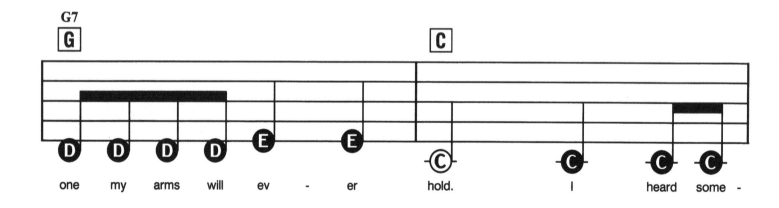

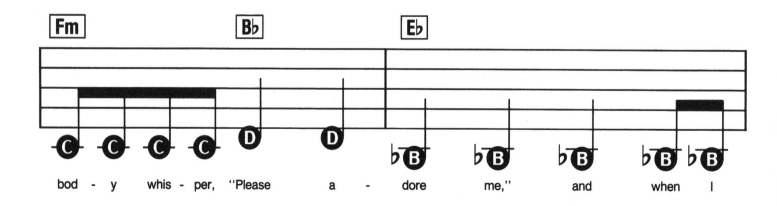

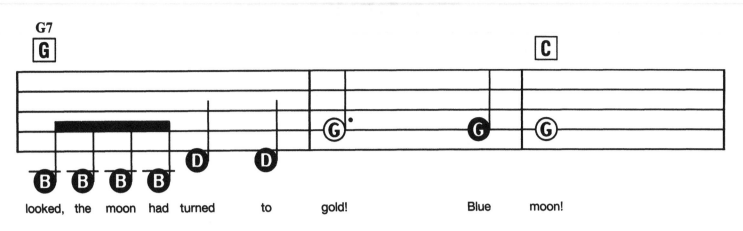

looked, the moon had turned to gold! Blue moon!

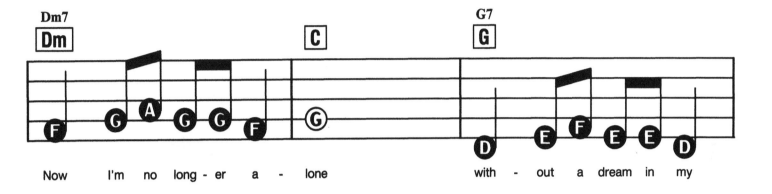

Now I'm no long-er a - lone with - out a dream in my

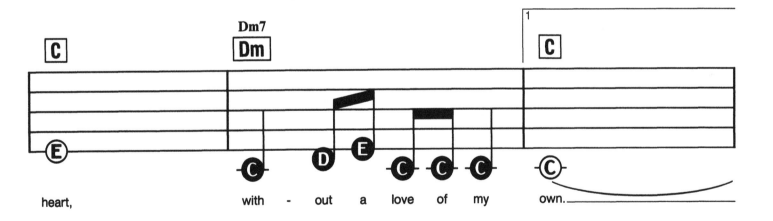

heart, with - out a love of my own.

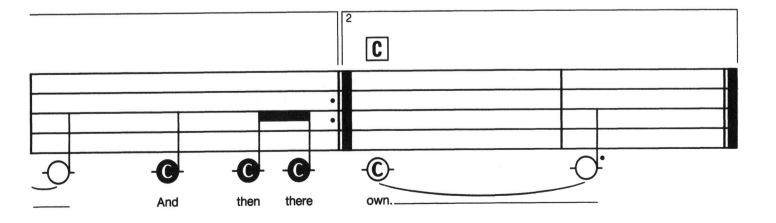

And then there own.

Mooning

Registration 2
Rhythm: Waltz or Rock Ballad

Lyric and Music by Warren Casey
and Jim Jacobs

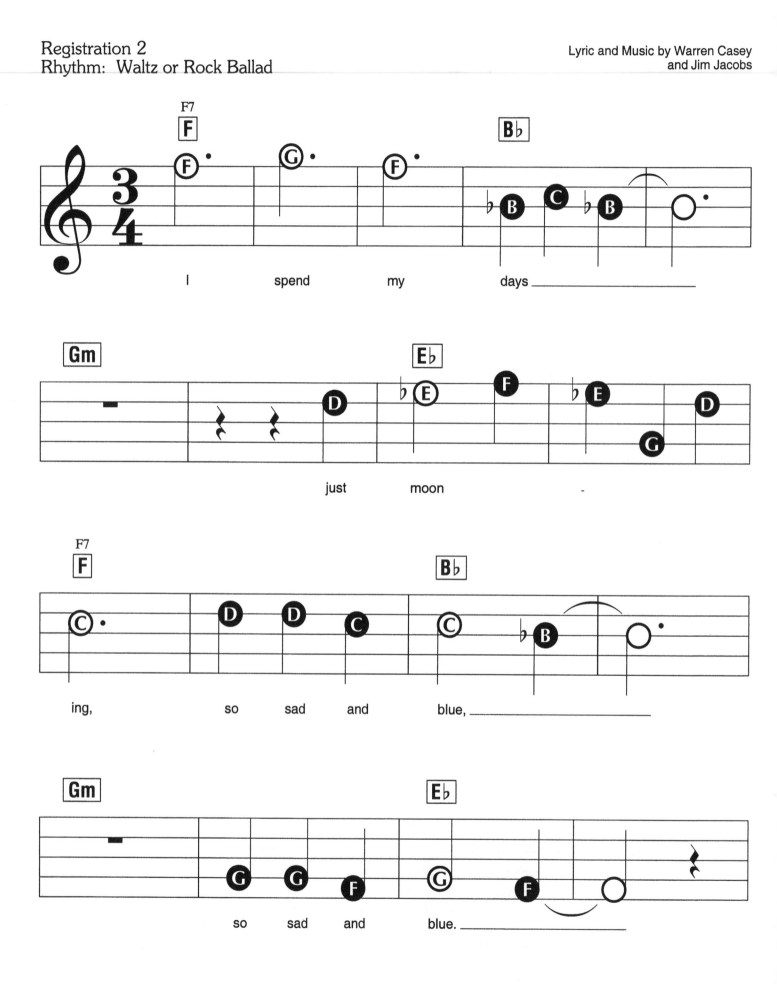

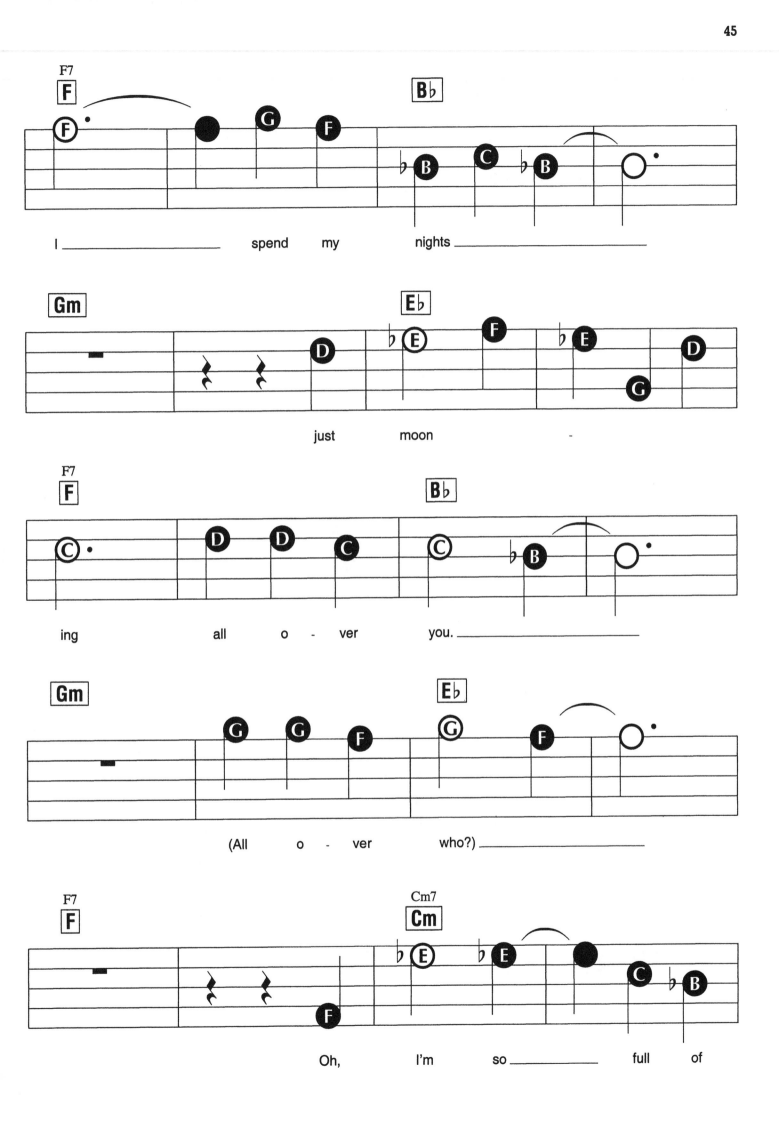

46

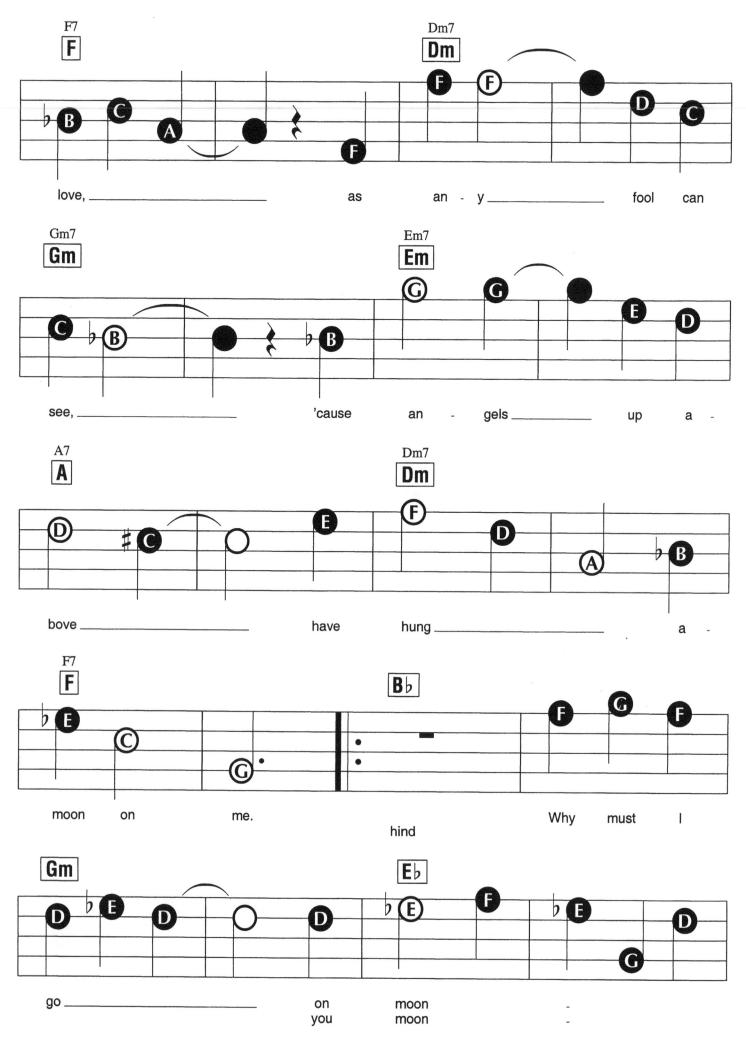

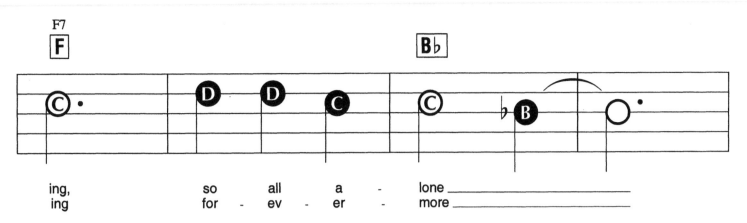

ing,   so   all   a - lone _____
ing   for - ev - er - more _____

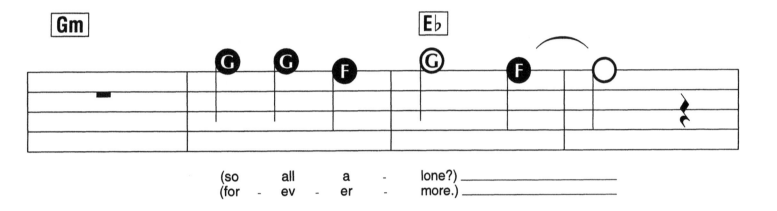

(so   all   a - lone?) _____
(for - ev - er - more.) _____

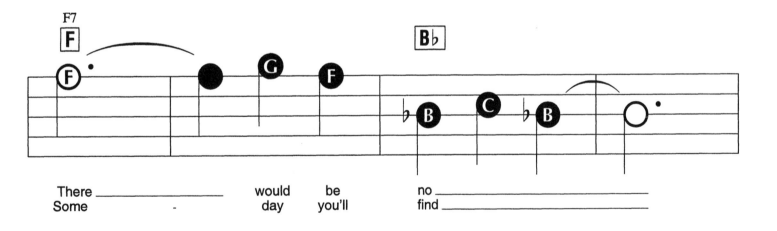

There _____ would be   no _____
Some - day you'll   find _____

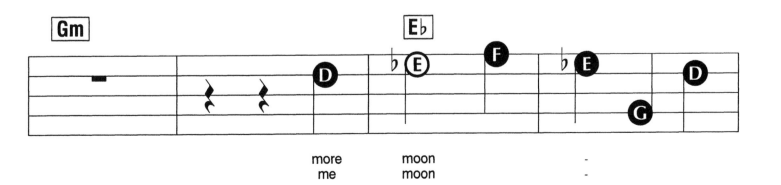

more   moon -
me   moon

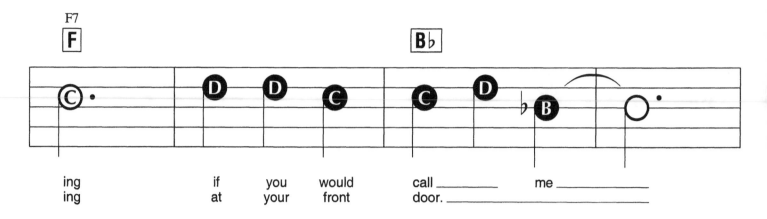

ing   if   you   would   call _____ me _____
ing   at   your   front   door. _____

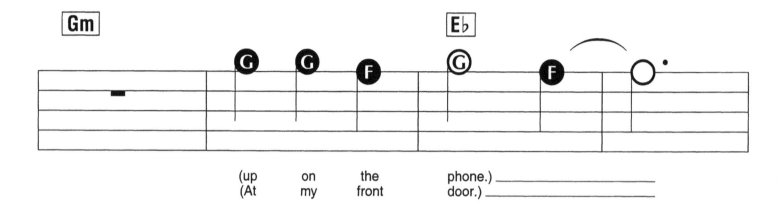

(up   on   the   phone.) _____
(At   my   front   door.) _____

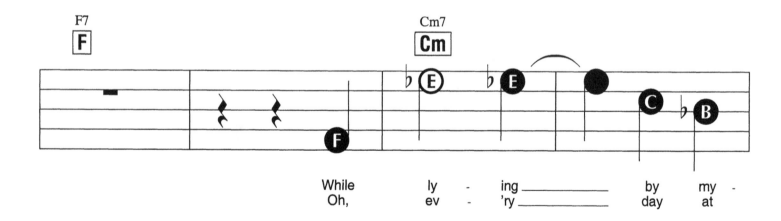

While   ly - ing _____ by   my -
Oh,   ev - 'ry _____ day   at

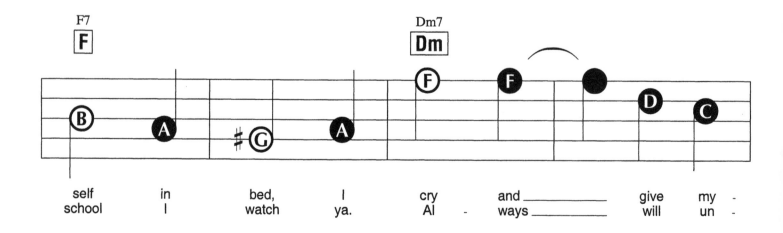

self   in   bed,   I   cry   and _____ give   my -
school   I   watch   ya.   Al - ways _____ will   un -

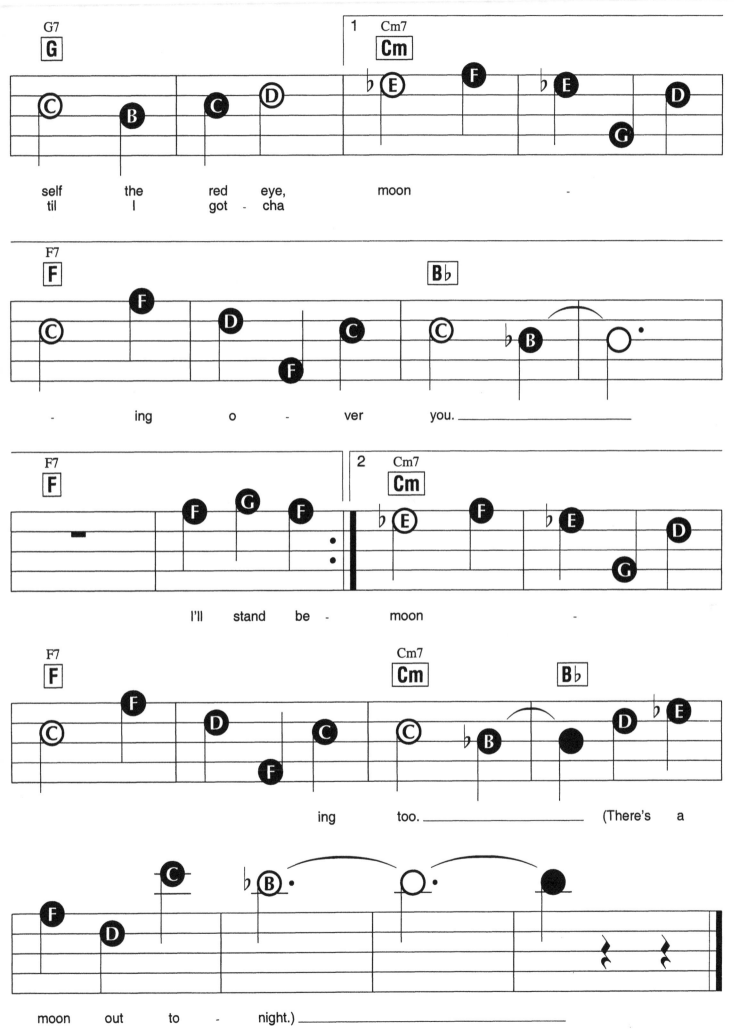

Alone at the Drive-In Movie

Registration 2
Rhythm: Waltz or Rock Ballad

Lyric and Music by Warren Casey
and Jim Jacobs

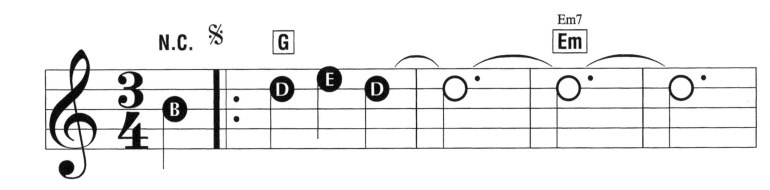

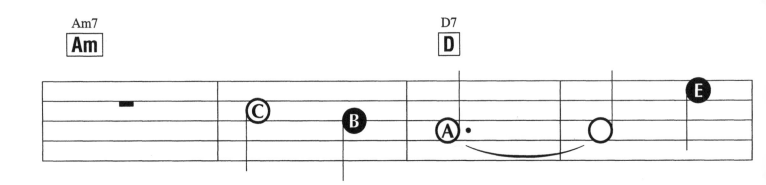

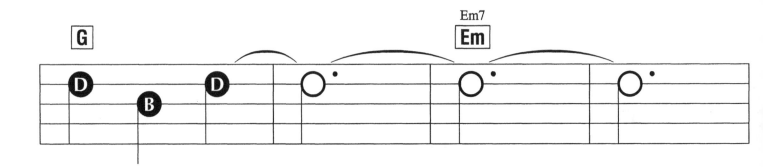

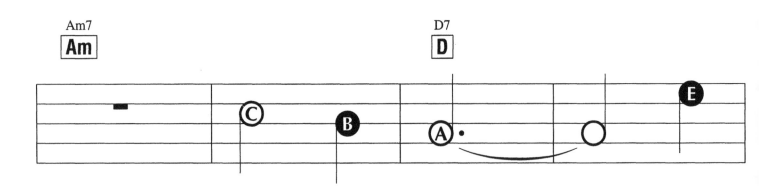

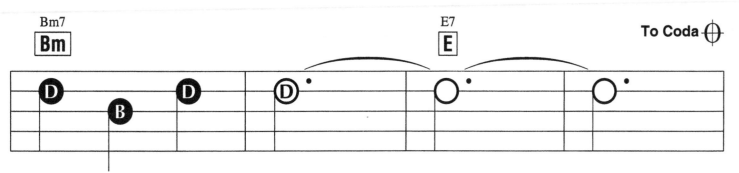

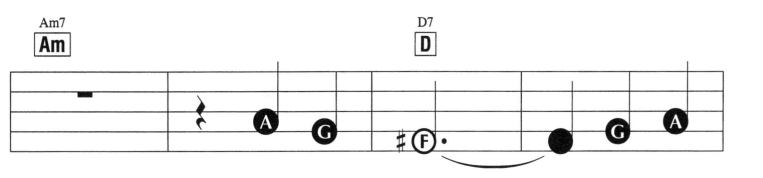

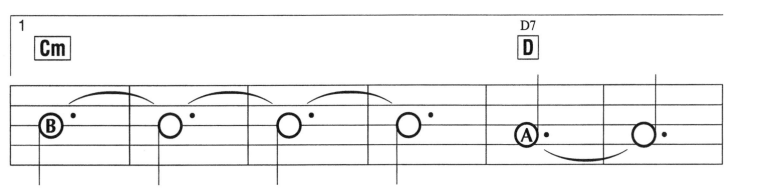

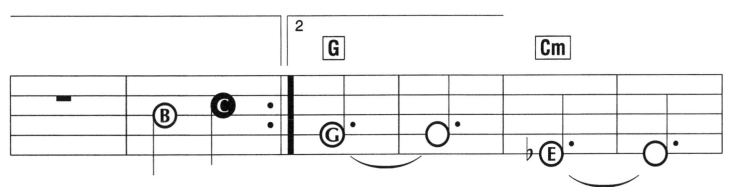

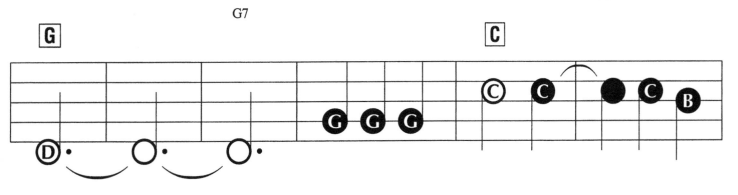

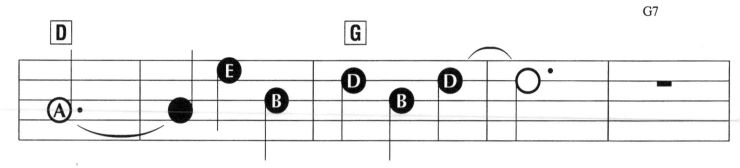

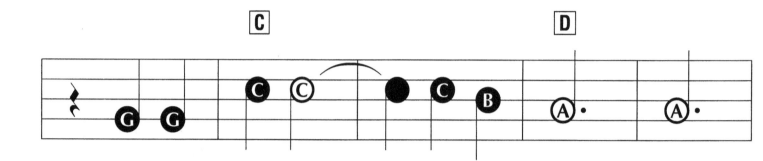

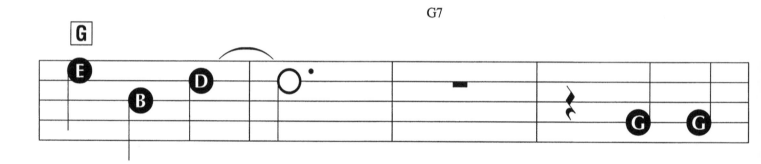

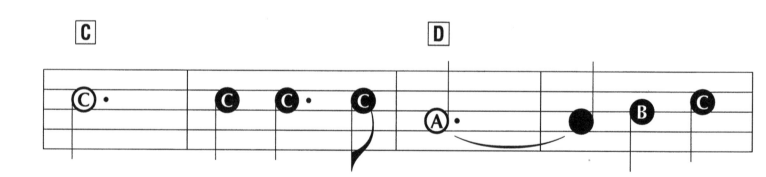

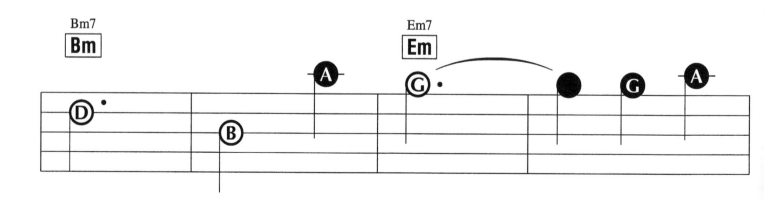

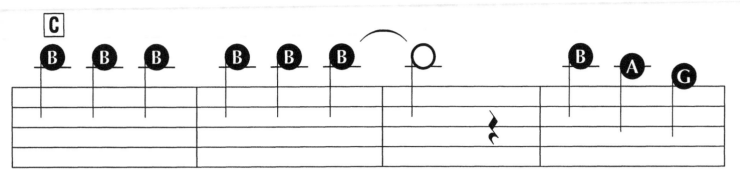

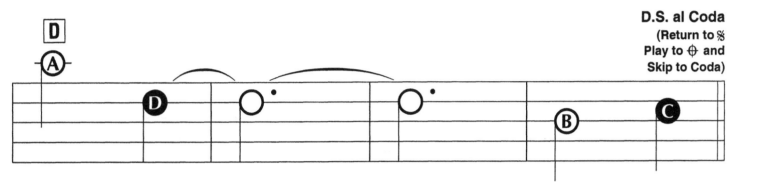

D.S. al Coda
(Return to %
Play to ⊕ and
Skip to Coda)

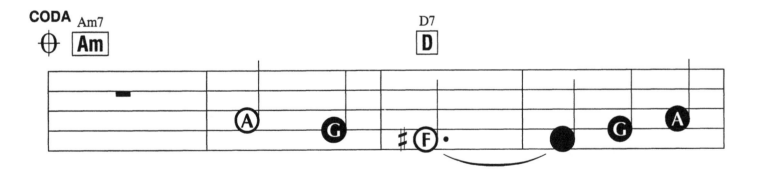

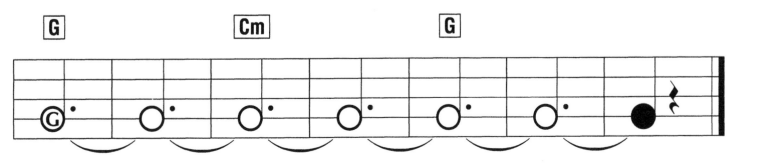

Rock and Roll Is Here to Stay

Registration 5
Rhythm: Rock 'n Roll

Words and Music by
David White

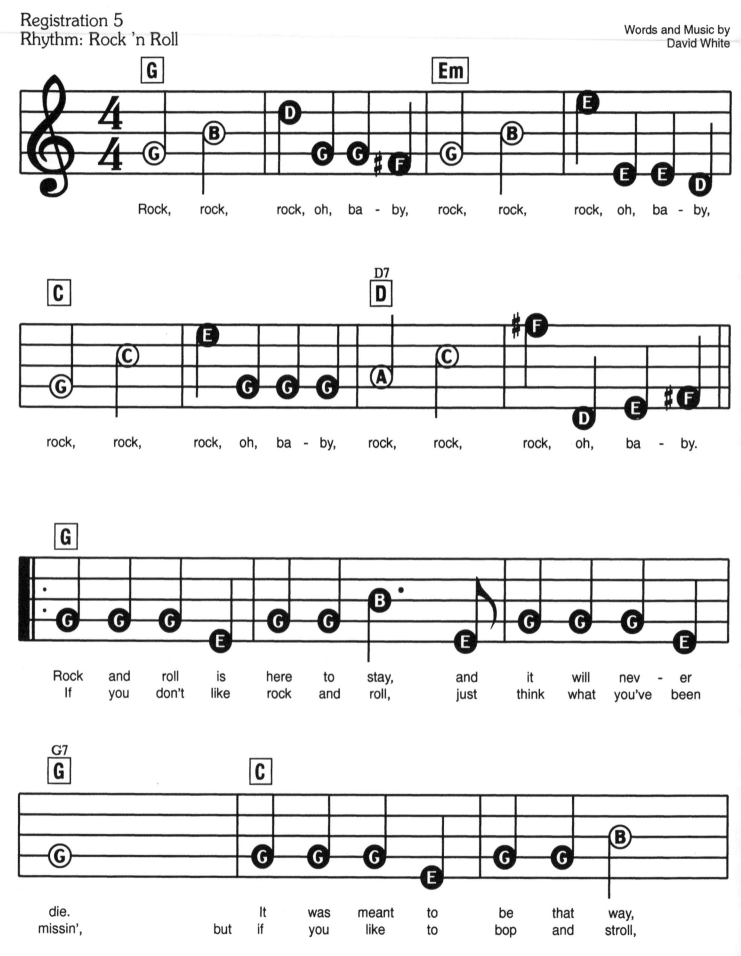

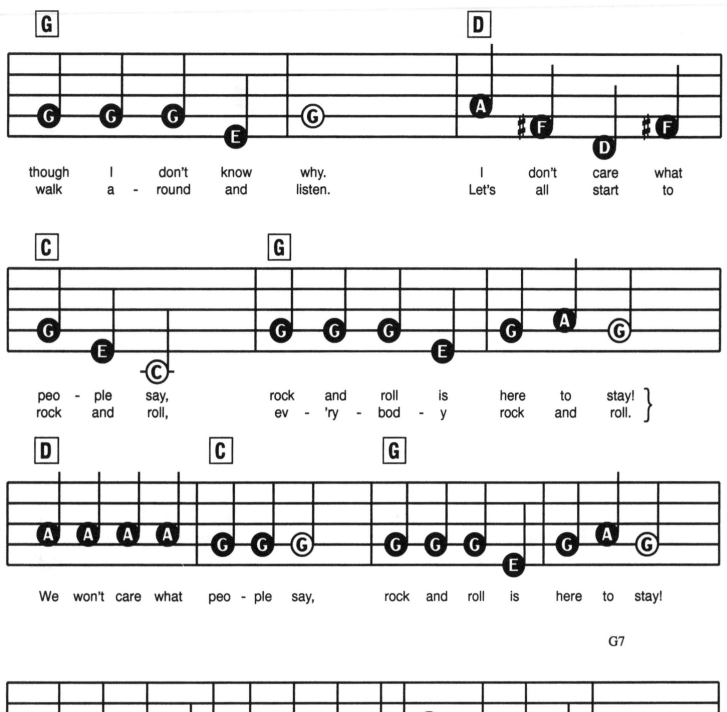

though   I   don't   know   why.   I   don't   care   what
walk   a - round   and   listen.   Let's   all   start   to

peo - ple   say,   rock   and   roll   is   here   to   stay!
rock   and   roll,   ev - 'ry - bod - y   rock   and   roll.

We   won't   care   what   peo - ple   say,   rock   and   roll   is   here   to   stay!

G7

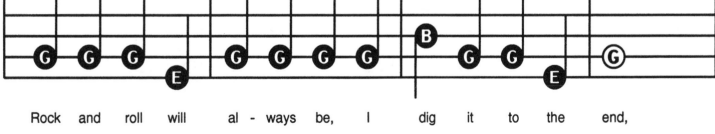

Rock   and   roll   will   al - ways   be,   I   dig   it   to   the   end,

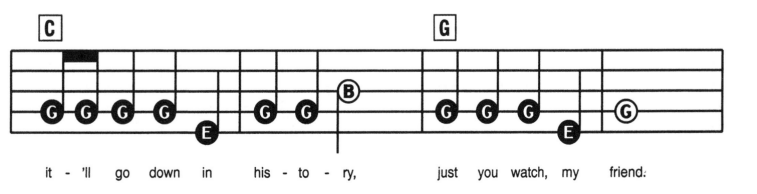

it - 'll   go   down   in   his - to - ry,   just   you   watch,   my   friend.

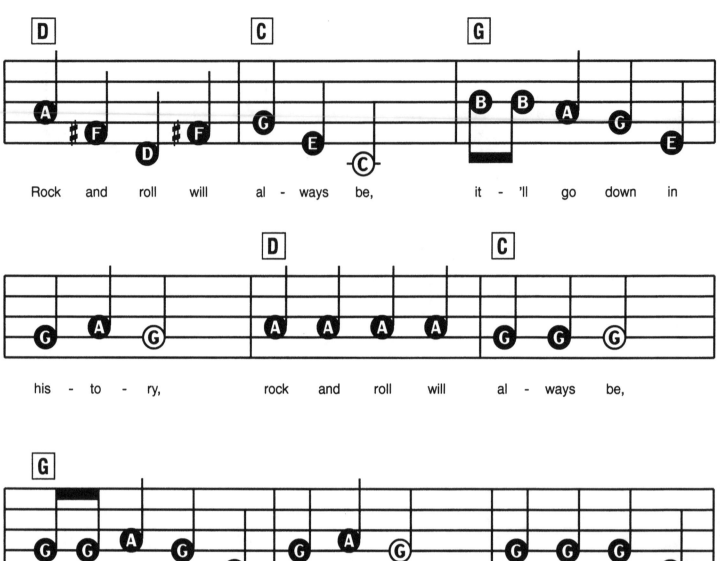

Rock and roll will al - ways be, it - 'll go down in

his - to - ry, rock and roll will al - ways be,

it - 'll go down in his - to - ry. Ev - 'ry - bod - y

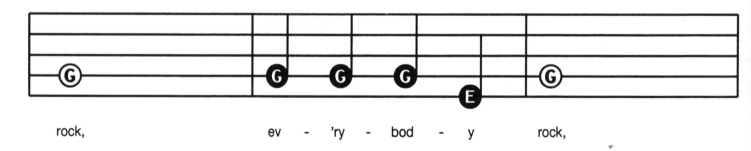

G7

rock, ev - 'ry - bod - y rock,

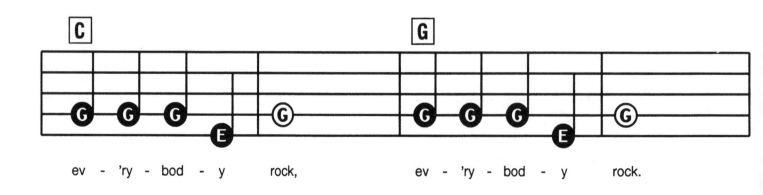

ev - 'ry - bod - y rock, ev - 'ry - bod - y rock.

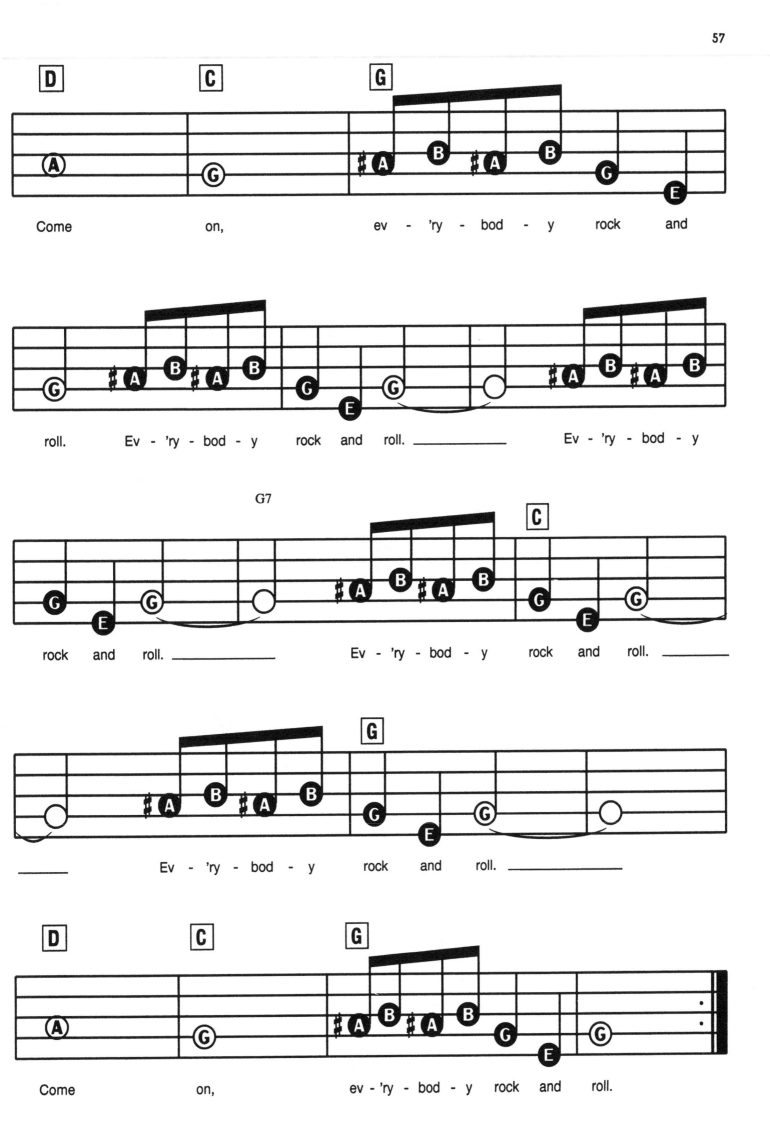

Those Magic Changes

Registration 8
Rhythm: Pops or 8 Beat

Lyric and Music by Warren Casey
and Jim Jacobs

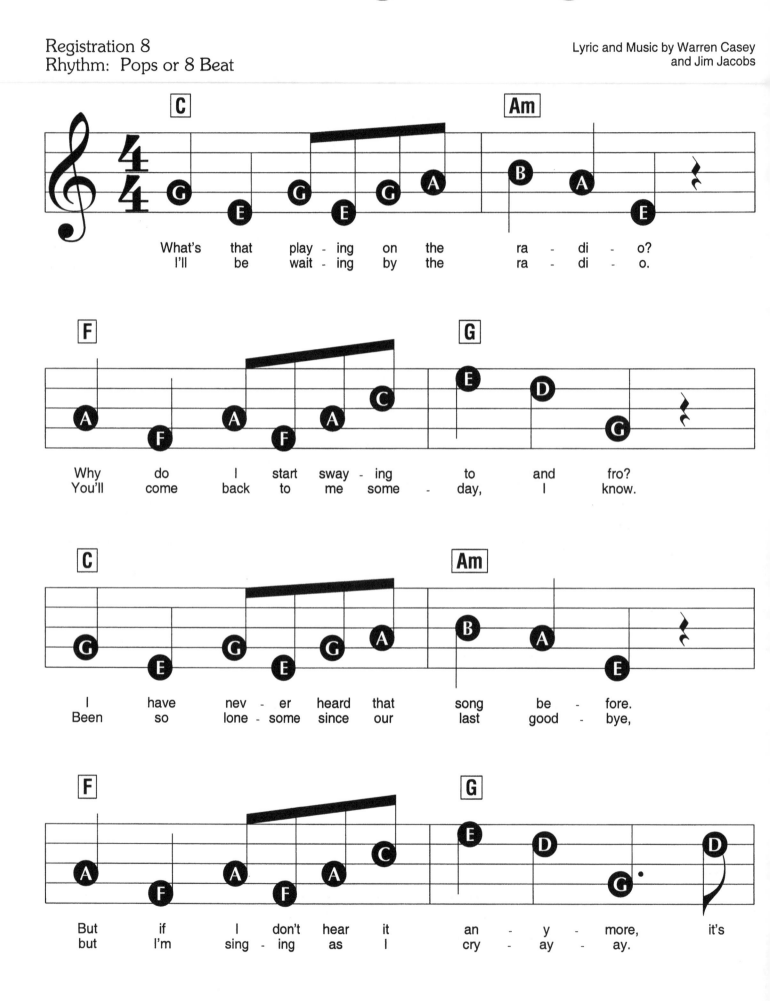

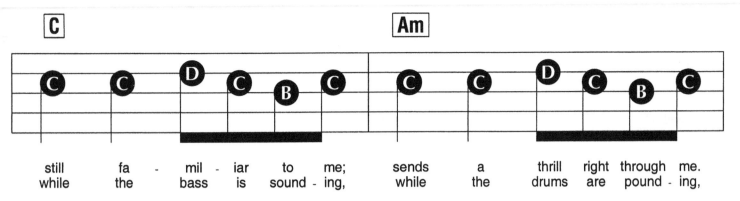

still fa - mil - iar to me; sends a thrill right through me.
while the bass is sound - ing, while the drums are pound - ing,

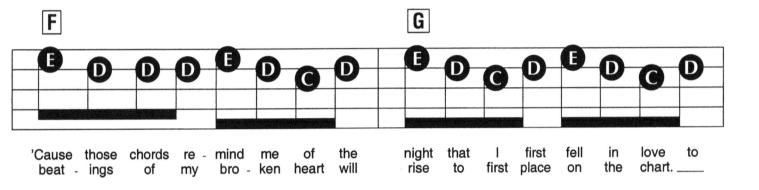

'Cause those chords re - mind me of the night that I first fell in love to
beat - ings of my bro - ken heart will rise to first place on the chart. ____

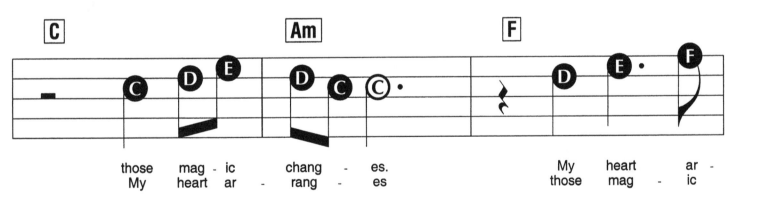

those mag - ic chang - es.
My heart ar - rang - es

My heart ar -
those mag - ic

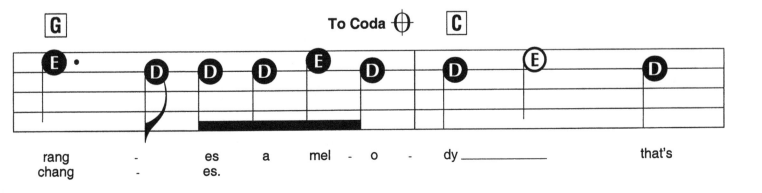

To Coda ⊕

rang - es a mel - o - dy _____ that's
chang - es.

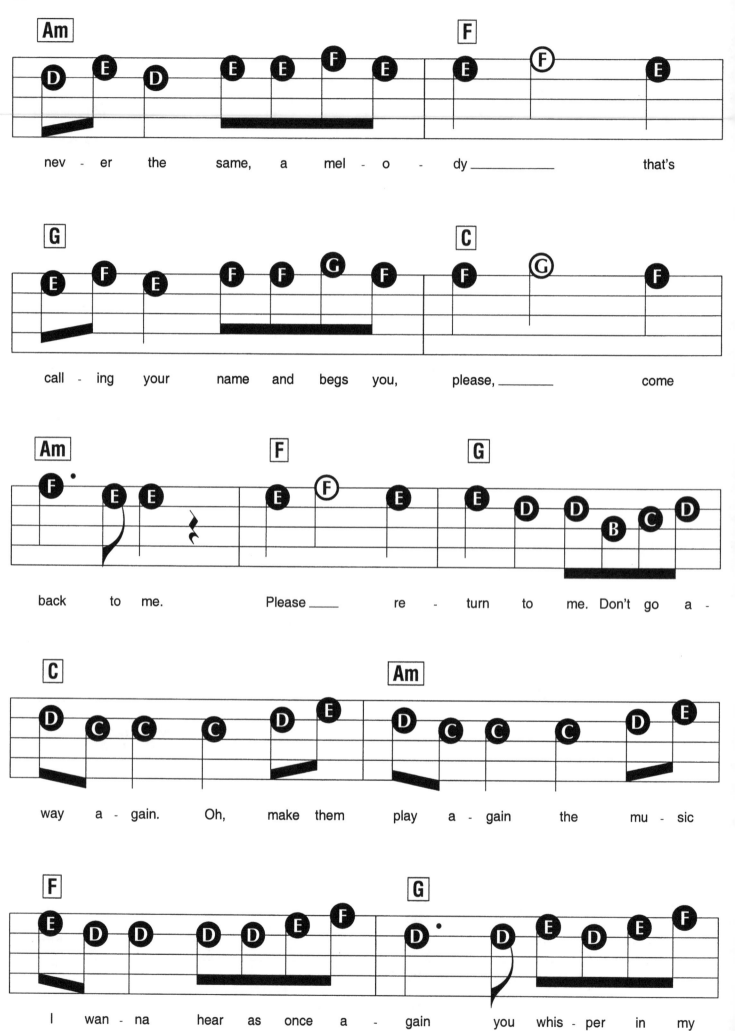

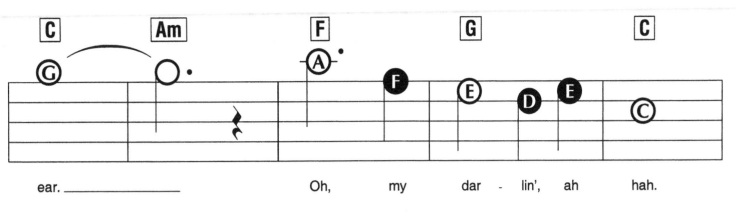

ear. _____ Oh, my dar - lin', ah hah.

D.C. al Coda
(Return to beginning
Play to ⊕ and
Skip to Coda)

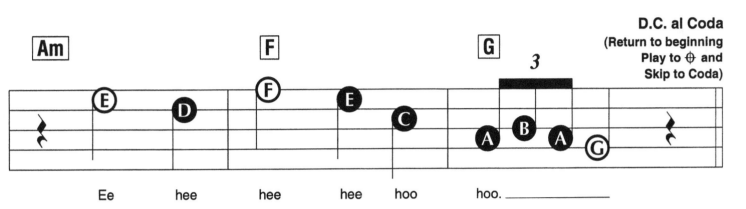

Ee hee hee hee hoo hoo. _____

CODA

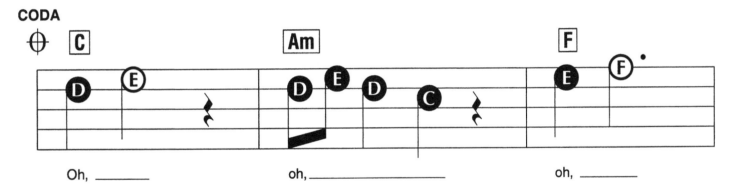

Oh, _____ oh, _____ oh, _____

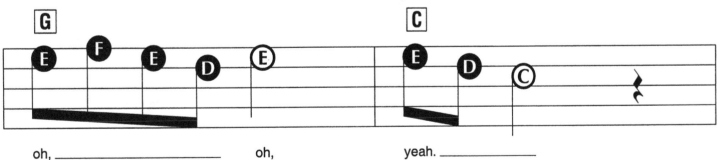

oh, _____ oh, yeah. _____

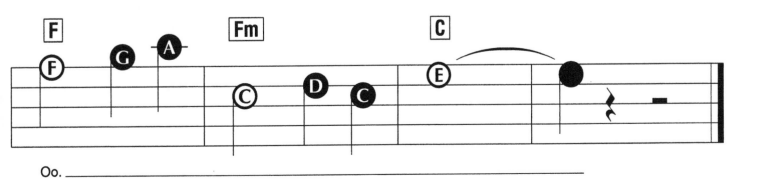

Oo. _____

Hound Dog

Registration 4
Rhythm: Rock 'n' Roll or Swing

Words and Music by Jerry Leiber
and Mike Stoller

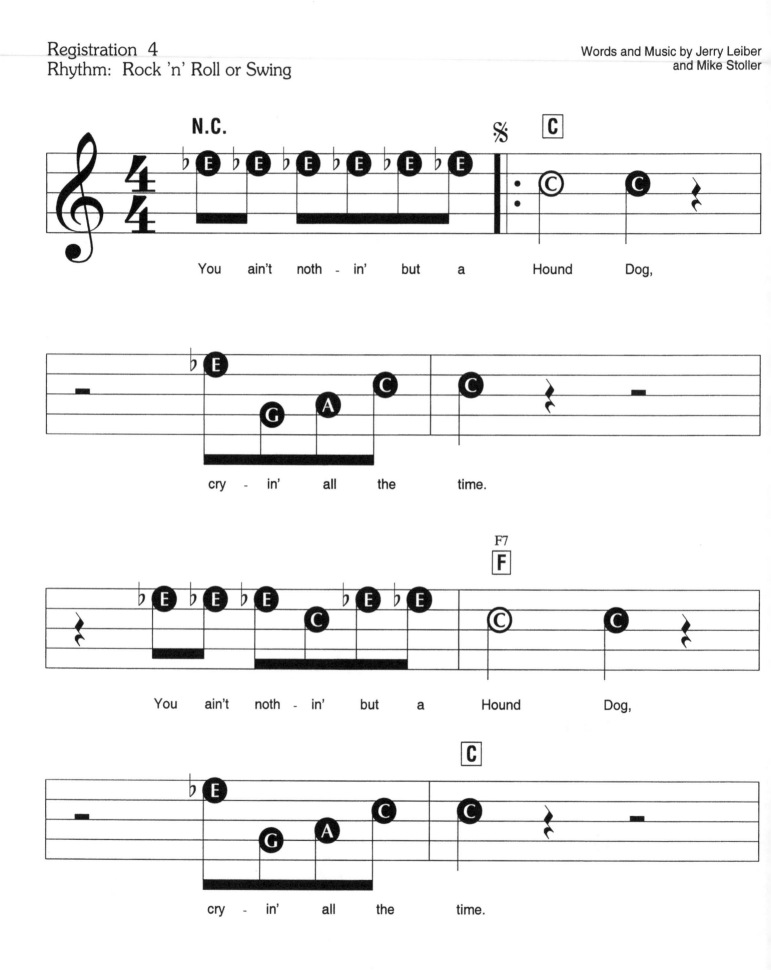

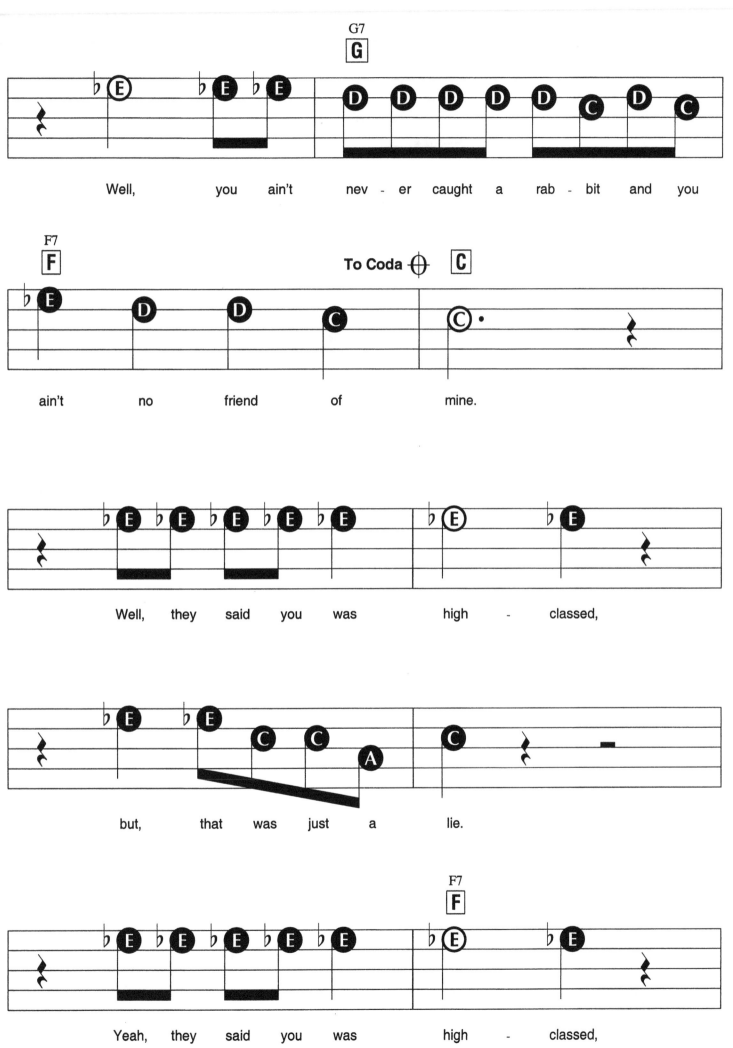

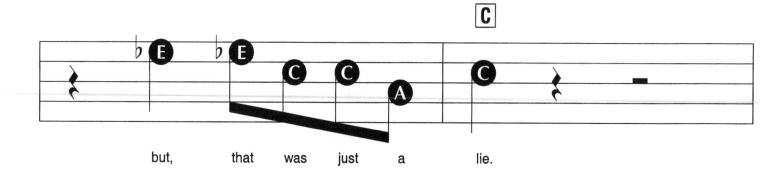

but, that was just a lie.

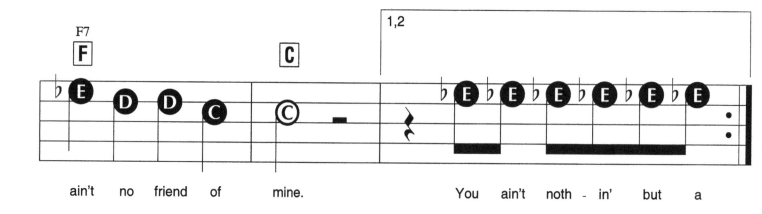

Yeah, you ain't nev - er caught a rab - bit and you

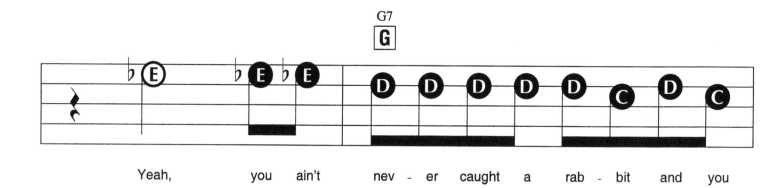

ain't no friend of mine. You ain't noth - in' but a

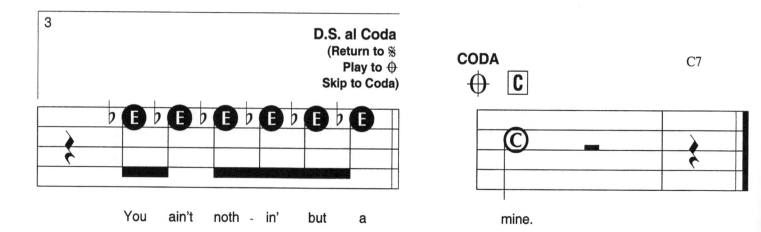

D.S. al Coda
(Return to %
Play to ⊕
Skip to Coda)

CODA

You ain't noth - in' but a

mine.

Born to Hand Jive

Registration 7
Rhythm: Funk or 16 Beat

Lyric and Music by Warren Casey
and Jim Jacobs

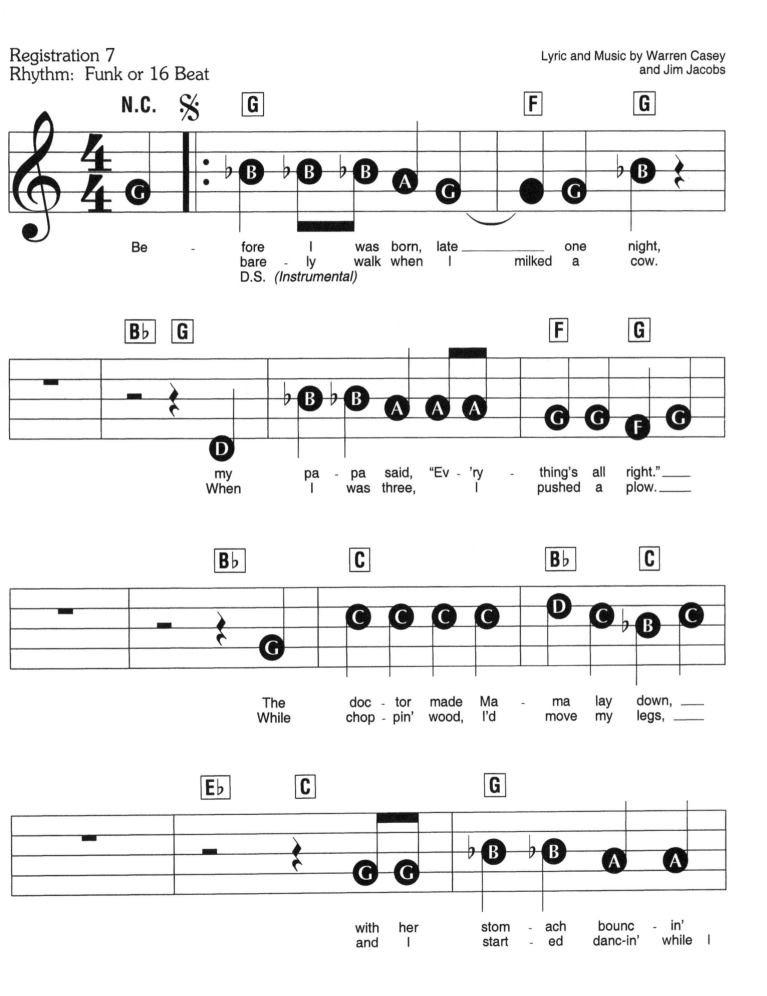

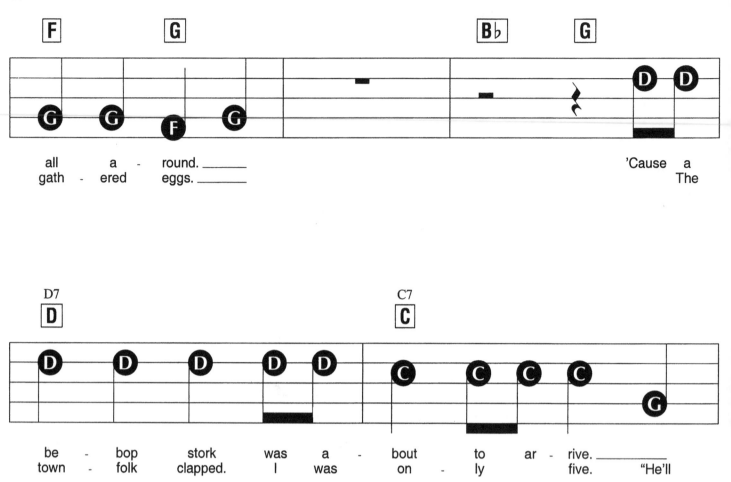

all a round. _____ 'Cause a
gath - ered eggs. _____ The

be - bop stork was a - bout to ar - rive. _____
town - folk clapped. I was on - ly five. "He'll

To Coda ⊕

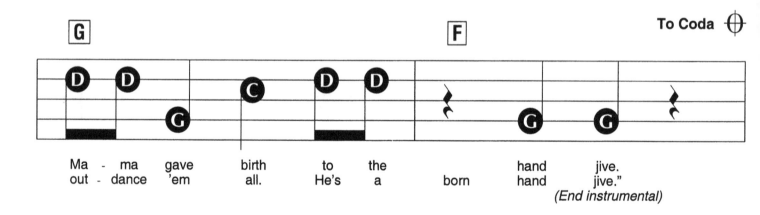

Ma - ma gave birth to the hand jive.
out - dance 'em all. He's a born hand jive."
(End instrumental)

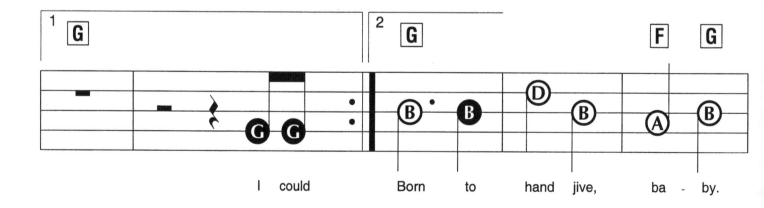

I could Born to hand jive, ba - by.

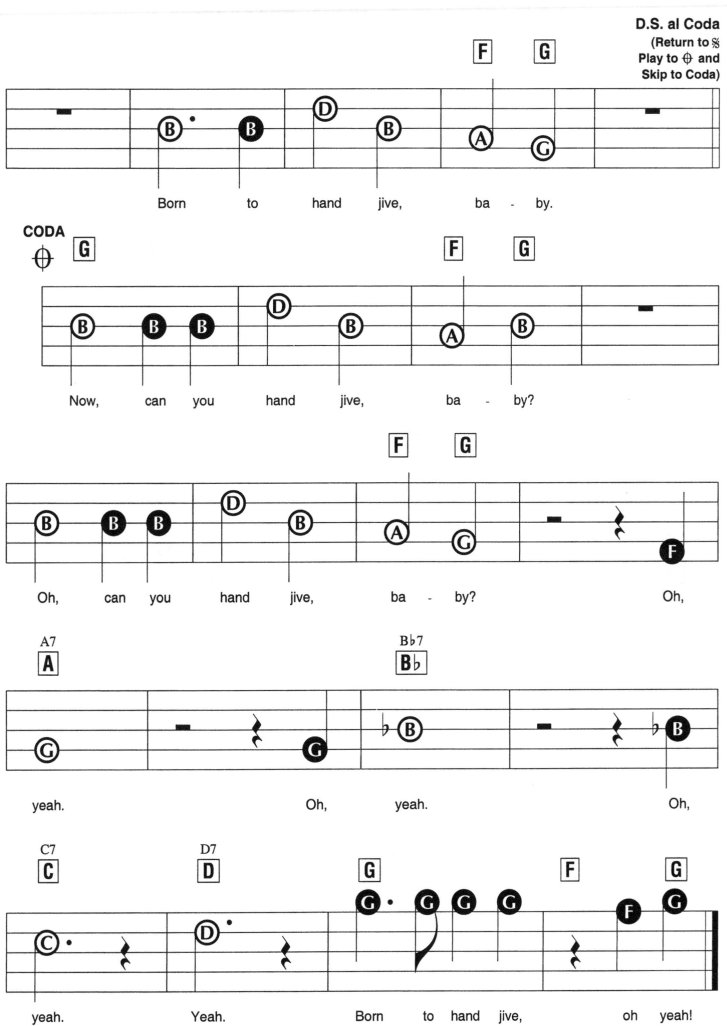

Tears on My Pillow

Registration 9
Rhythm: Slow Rock or Shuffle

Words and Music by Sylvester Bradford
and Al Lewis

You   don't   re - mem - ber   me   but   I   re - mem - ber   you
If   we   could   start   a - new   I   would - n't   hes - i - tate
Be - fore   you   go   a - way   my   dar - ling   think   of   me

'Twas   not   so   long   a - go   you   broke   my   heart   in   two
I'd   glad - ly   take   you   back   and   tempt   the   hand   of   fate
There   may   be   still   a   chance   to   end   my   mis - er - y

Tears   on   my   pil - low   pain   in   my   heart _____ Caused _ by

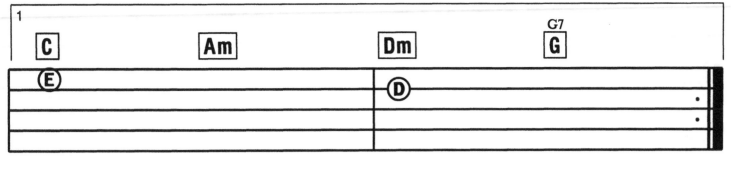

you. _____

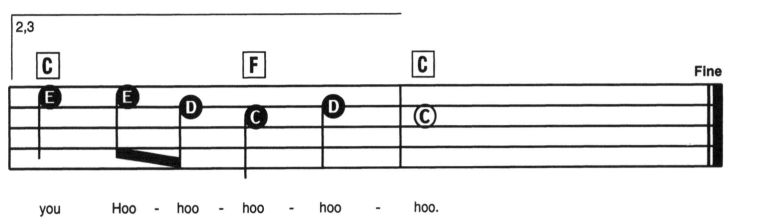

you   Hoo - hoo - hoo - hoo - hoo.

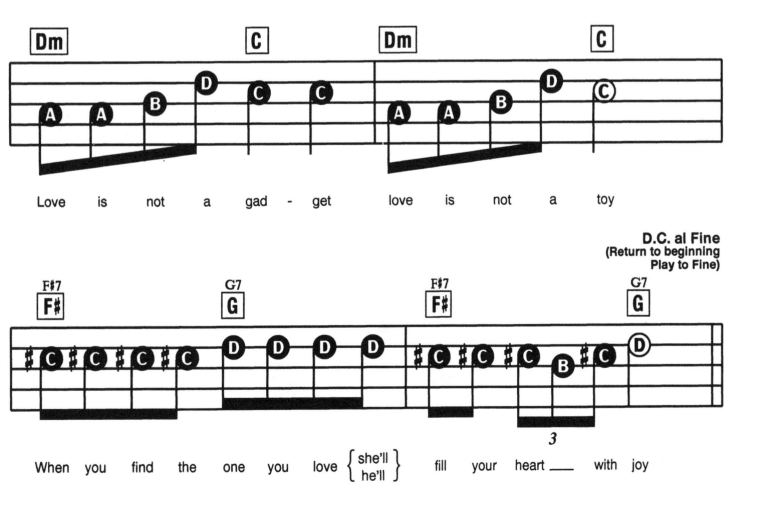

Dm   C   Dm   C

Love   is   not   a   gad - get   love   is   not   a   toy

D.C. al Fine
(Return to beginning
Play to Fine)

When   you   find   the   one   you   love { she'll / he'll }   fill   your   heart ___ with   joy

Freddy, My Love

Registration 8
Rhythm: Rock Ballad or Waltz

Lyric and Music by Warren Casey
and Jim Jacobs

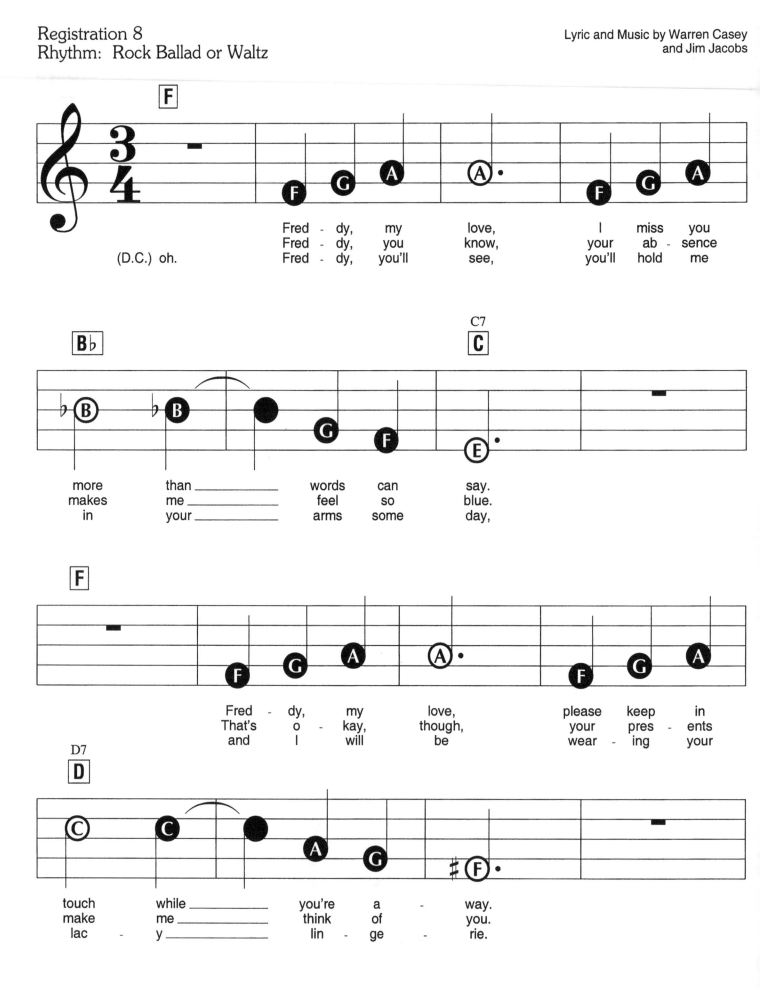

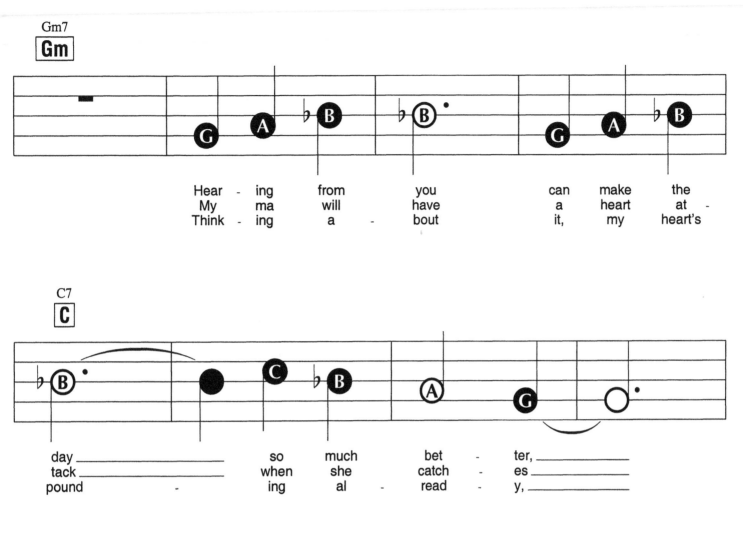

Gm7 | Gm

Hear - ing from you can make the
My ma will have a heart at -
Think - ing a - bout it, my heart's

C7 | C

day _____ so much bet - ter, _____
tack _____ when she catch - es _____
pound - ing al - read - y, _____

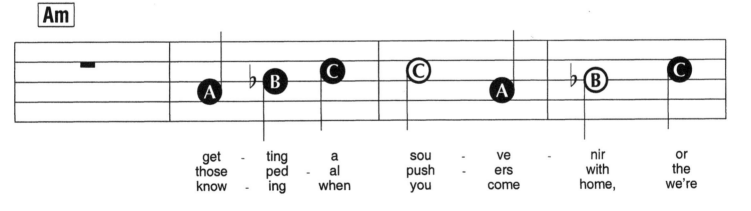

Am

get - ting a sou - ve - nir or
those ped - al push - ers with the
know - ing when you come home, we're

D7 | D

may - be a let - ter. _____
black _____ leath - er patch - es.
bound _____ to go stead - y, _____

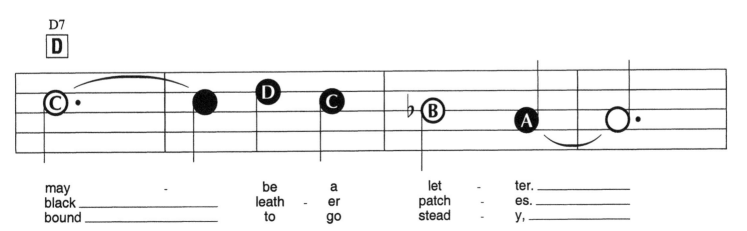

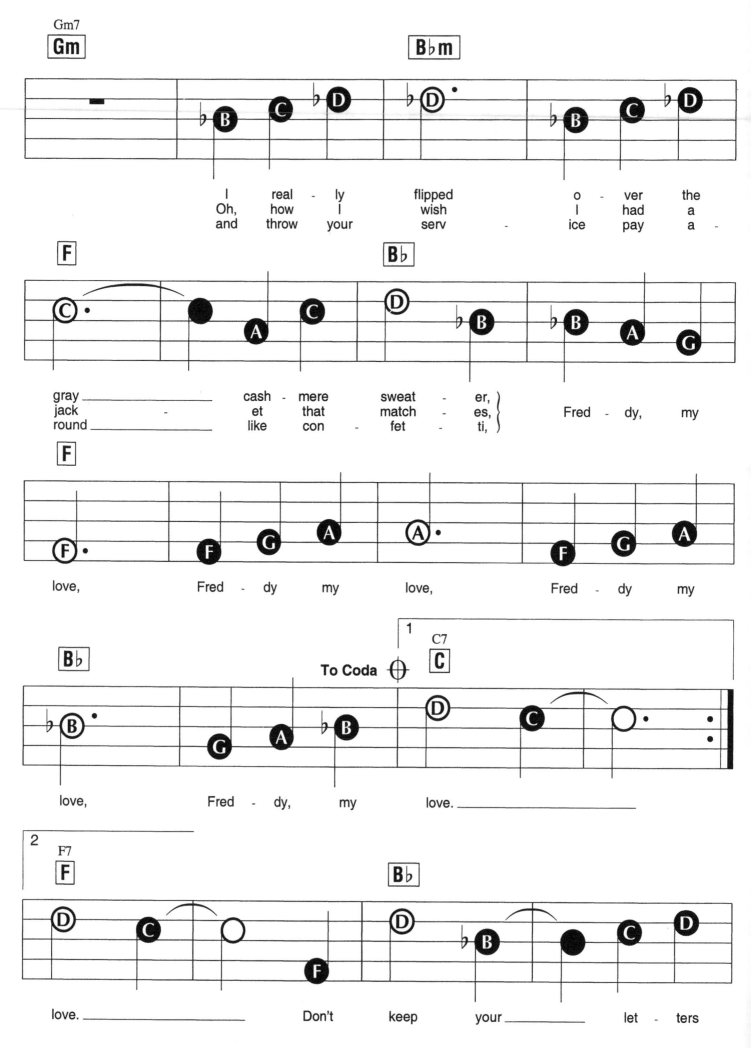

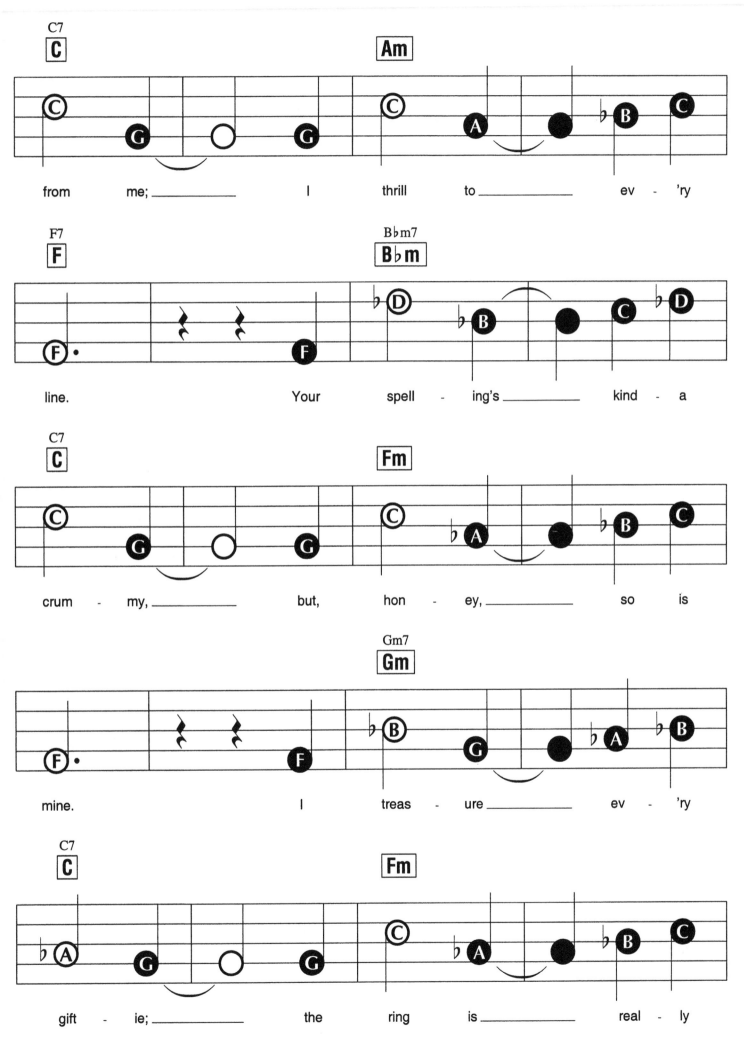

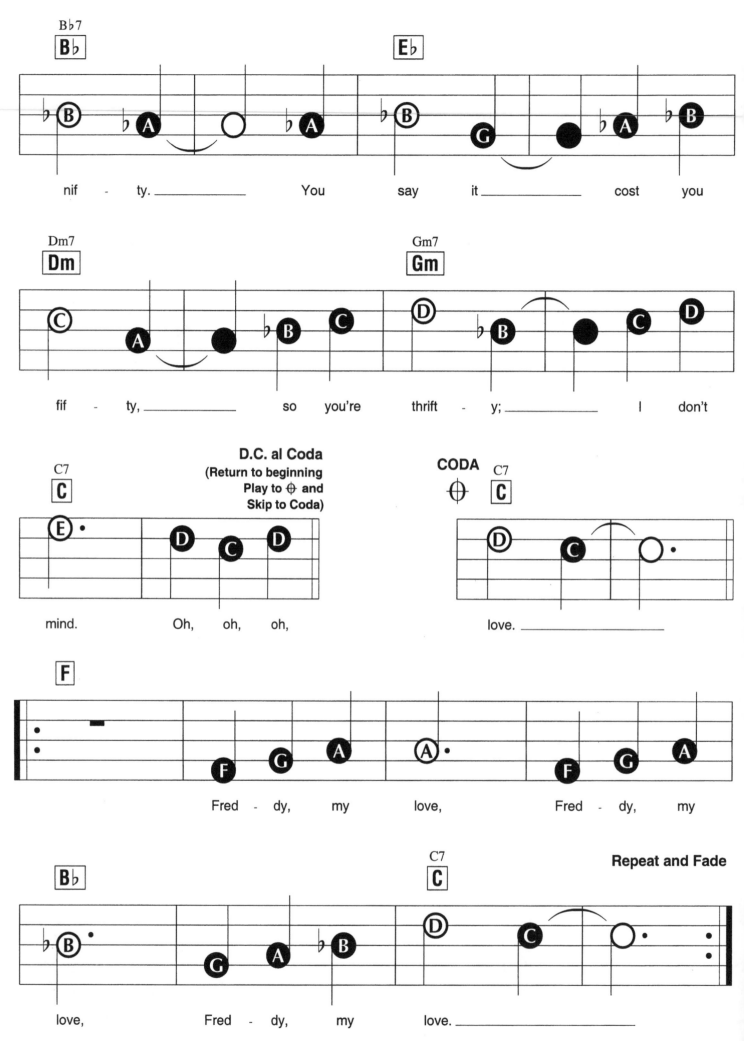

Rock 'n' Roll Party Queen

Registration 9
Rhythm: Rock or 8 Beat

Lyric and Music by Warren Casey
and Jim Jacobs

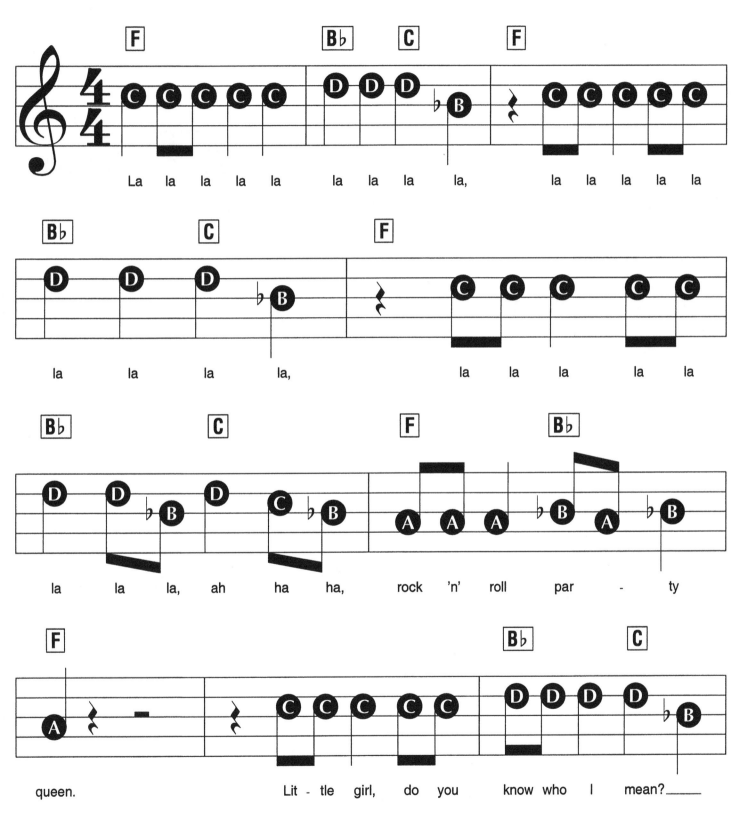

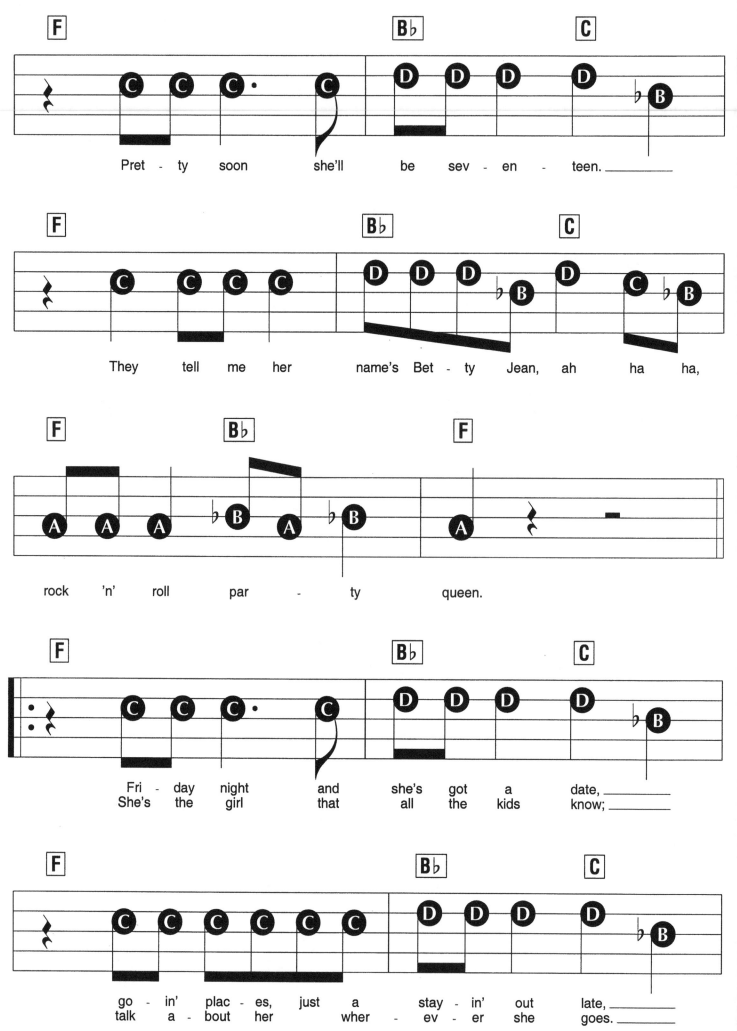

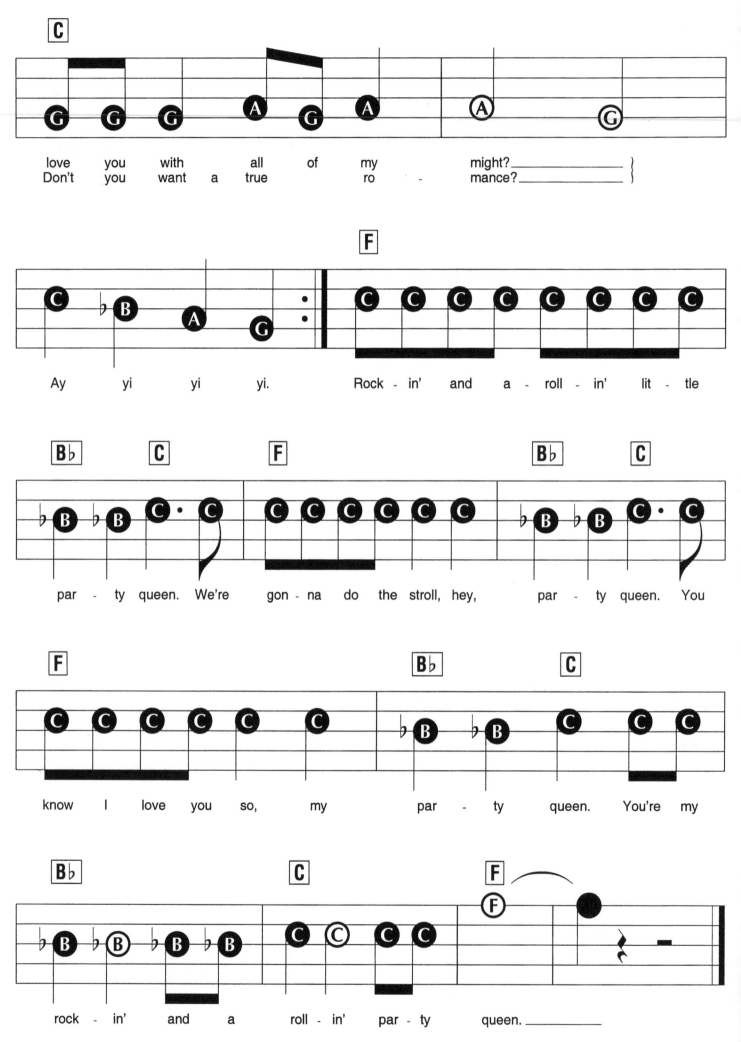

There Are Worse Things I Could Do

Registration 1
Rhythm: Rock Ballad or Waltz

Lyric and Music by Warren Casey
and Jim Jacobs

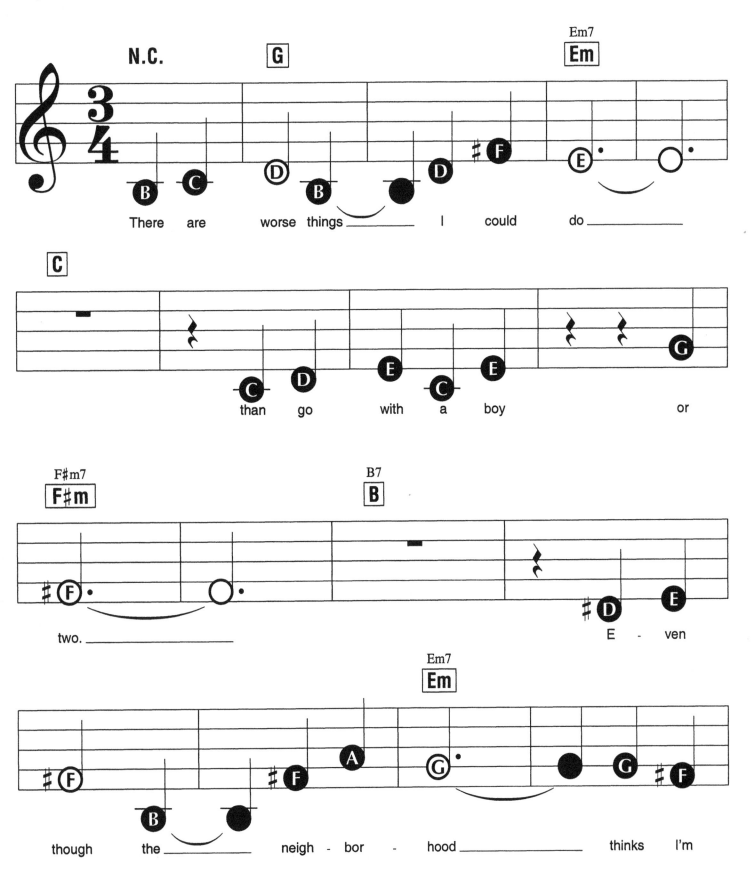

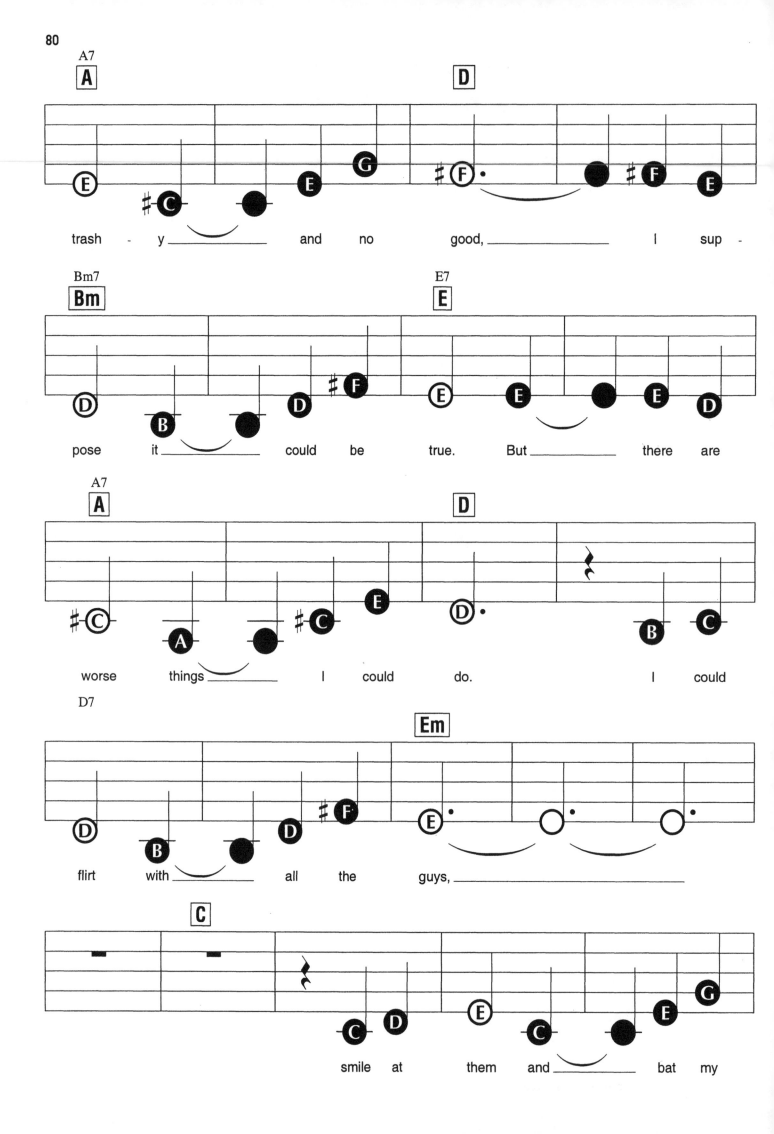

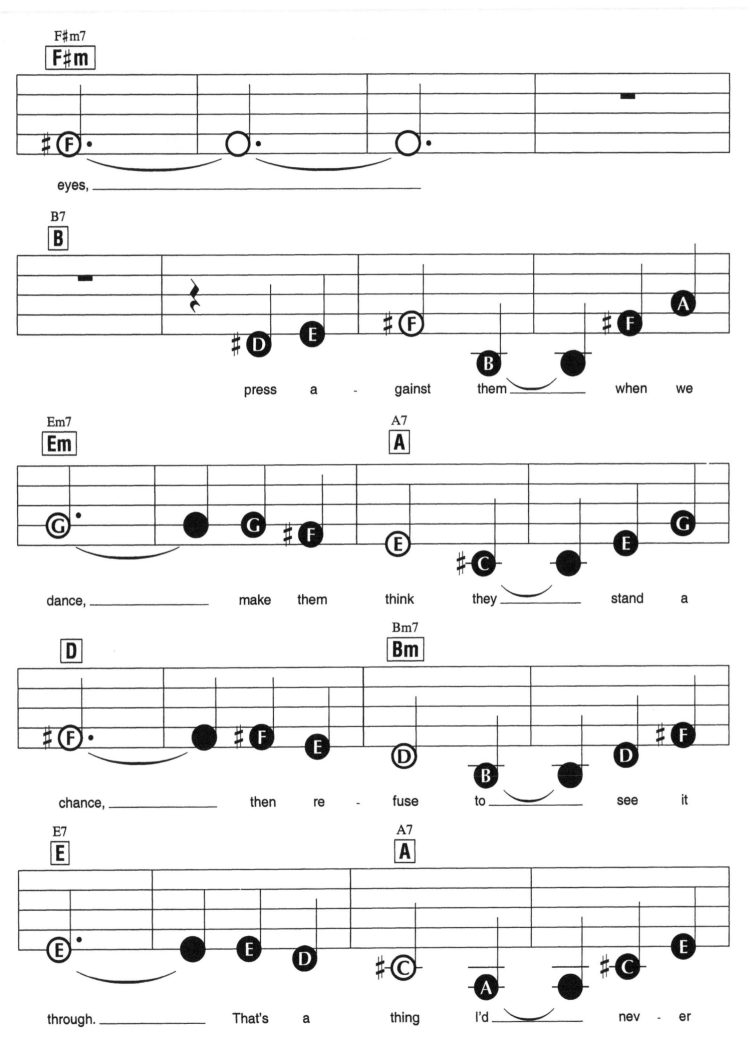

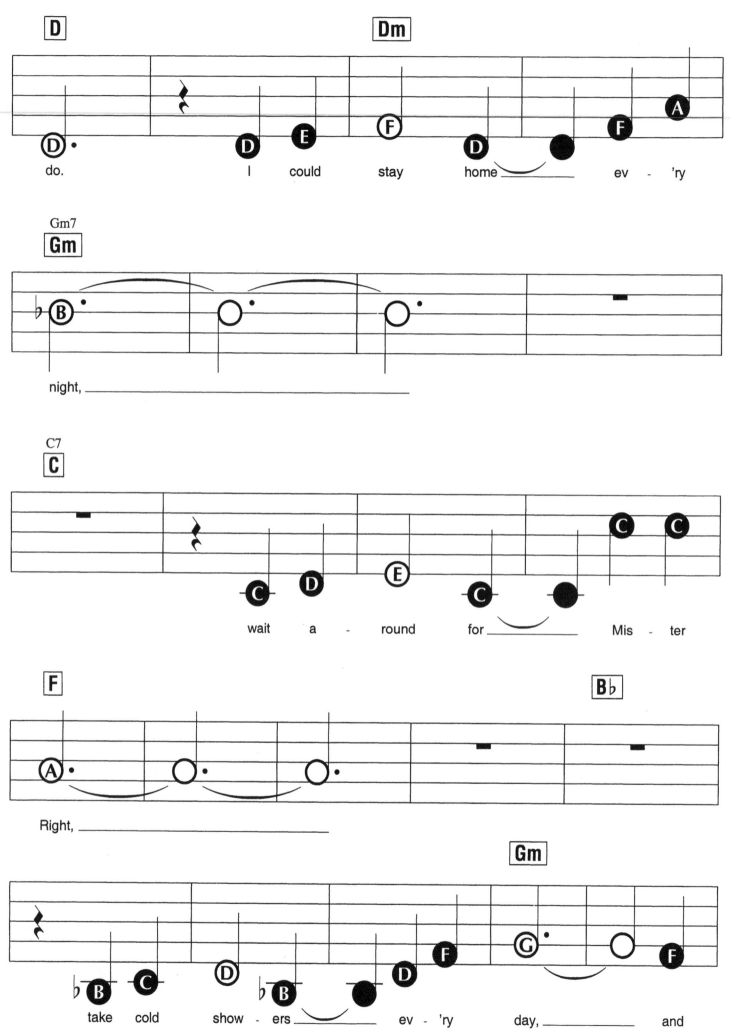

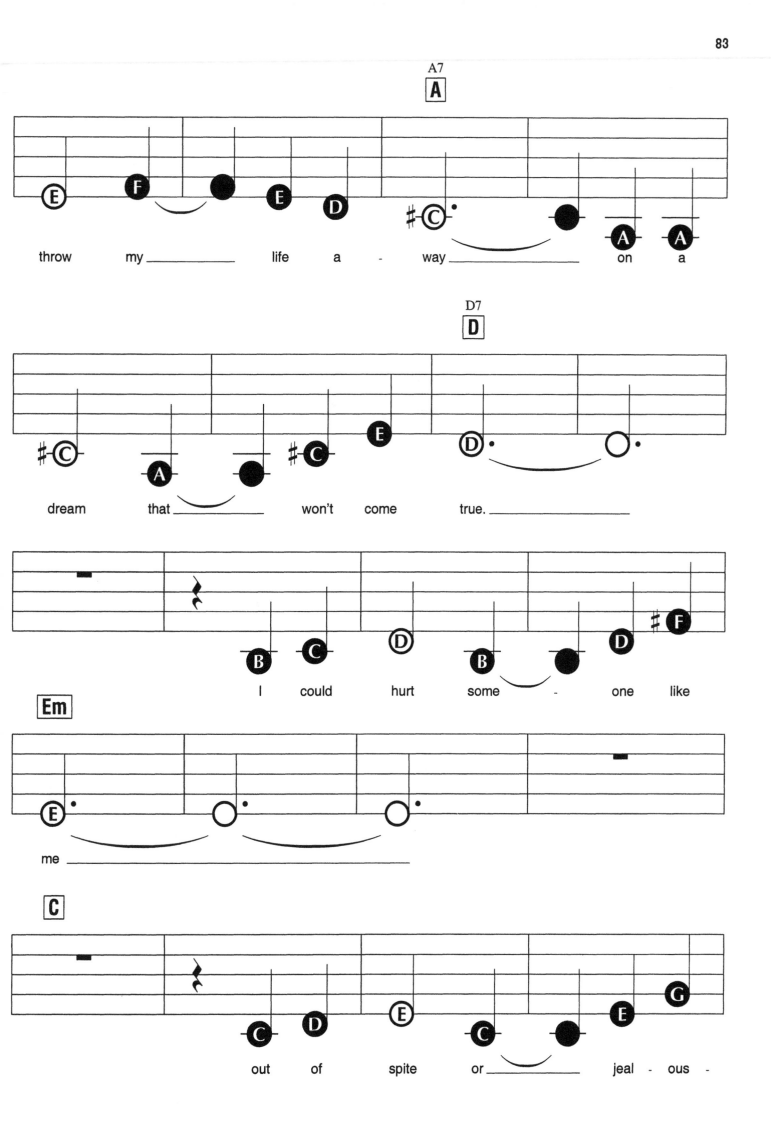

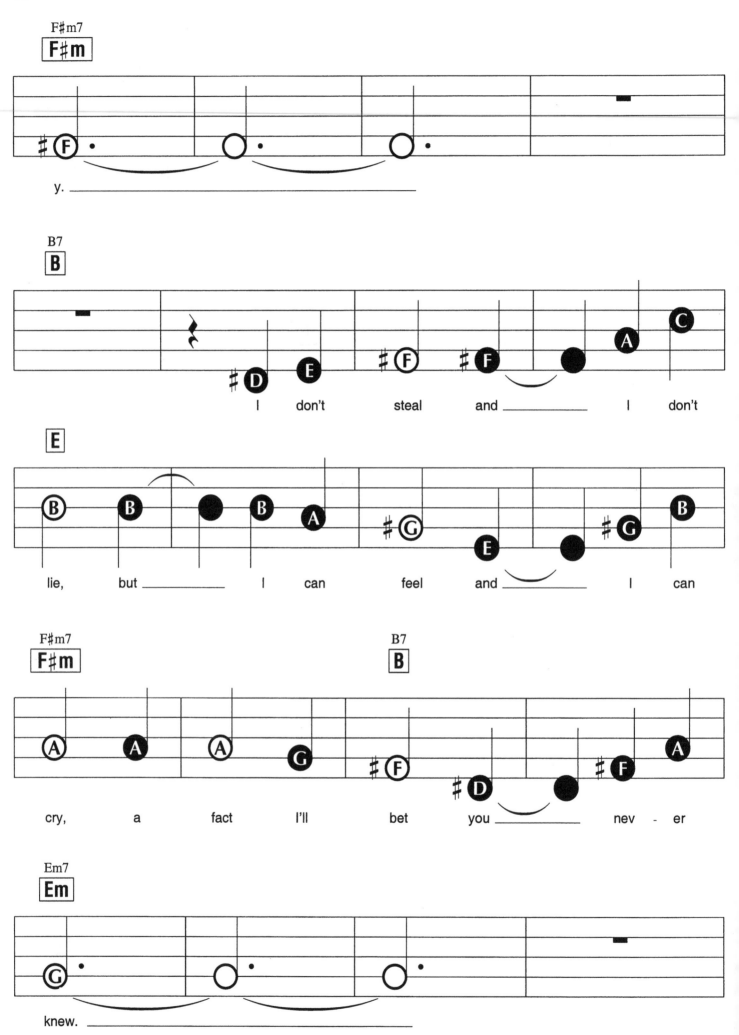

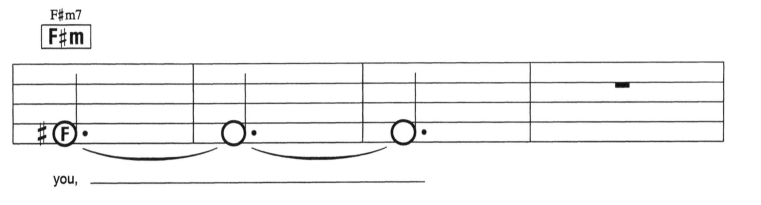

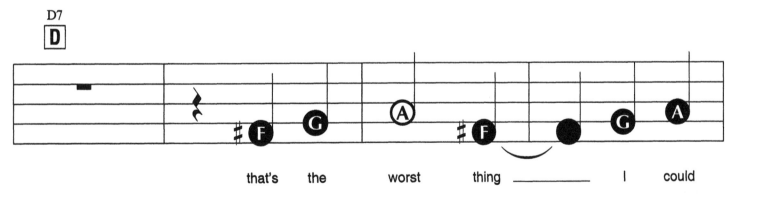

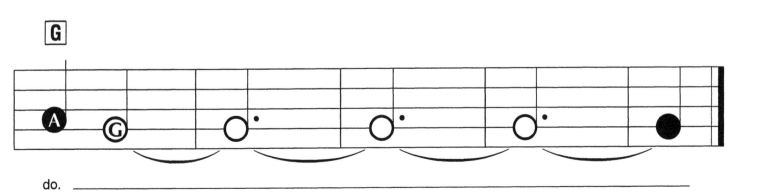

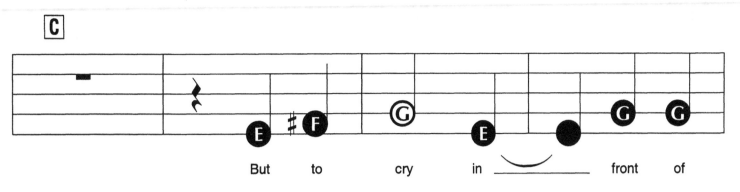

85

Love Is a Many-Splendored Thing

Registration 9
Rhythm: Swing

Words by Paul Francis Webster
Music by Sammy Fain

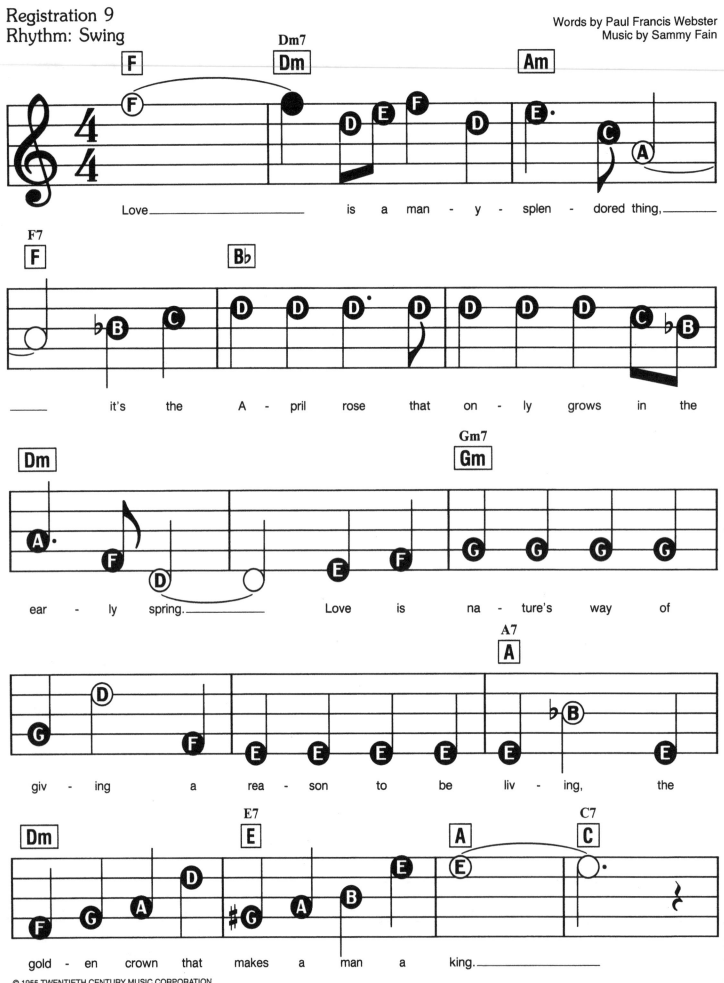

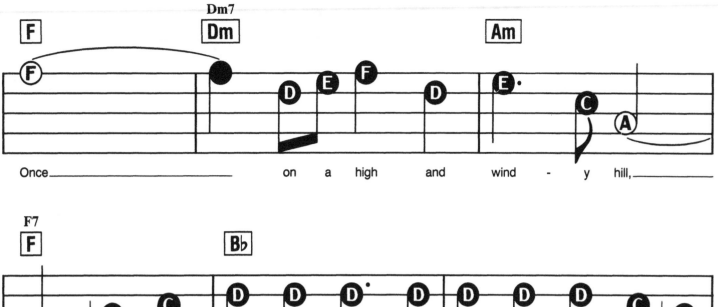

Once_____ on a high and wind - y hill, _____

_____ in the morn - ing mist two lov - ers kissed and the

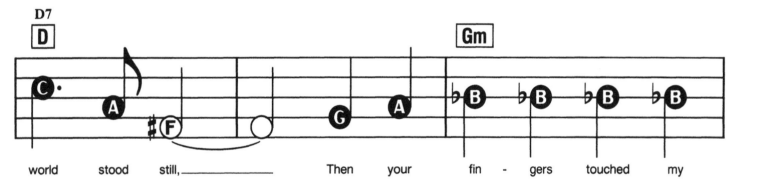

world stood still, _____ Then your fin - gers touched my

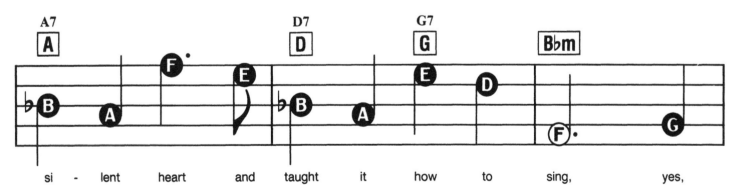

si - lent heart and taught it how to sing, yes,

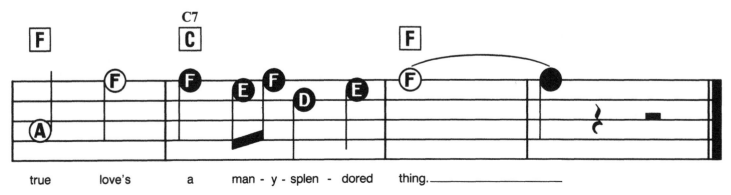

true love's a man - y - splen - dored thing. _____

We Go Together

Registration 5
Rhythm: Rock or Pops

Lyric and Music by Warren Casey
and Jim Jacobs

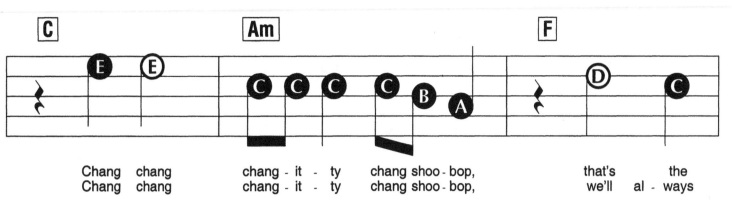

Chang chang   chang - it - ty   chang shoo - bop,   that's   the
Chang chang   chang - it - ty   chang shoo - bop,   we'll   al - ways

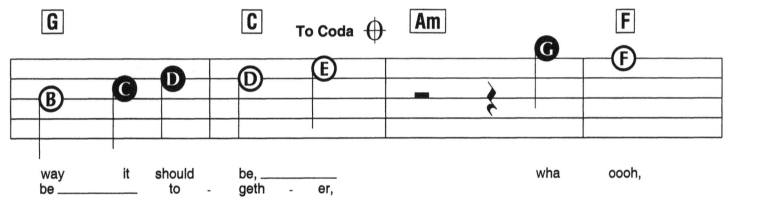

way   it   should   be, _____   wha   oooh,
be _____   to - geth - er,

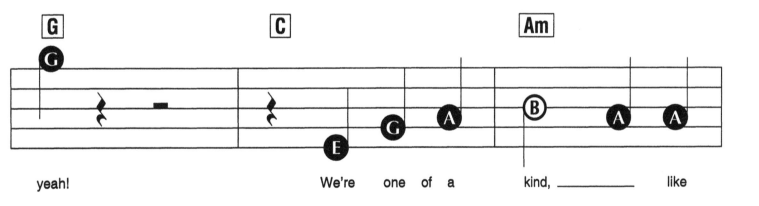

yeah!   We're   one   of   a   kind, _____   like

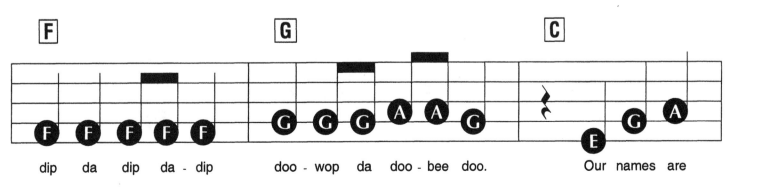

dip   da   dip   da - dip   doo - wop   da   doo - bee   doo.   Our   names   are

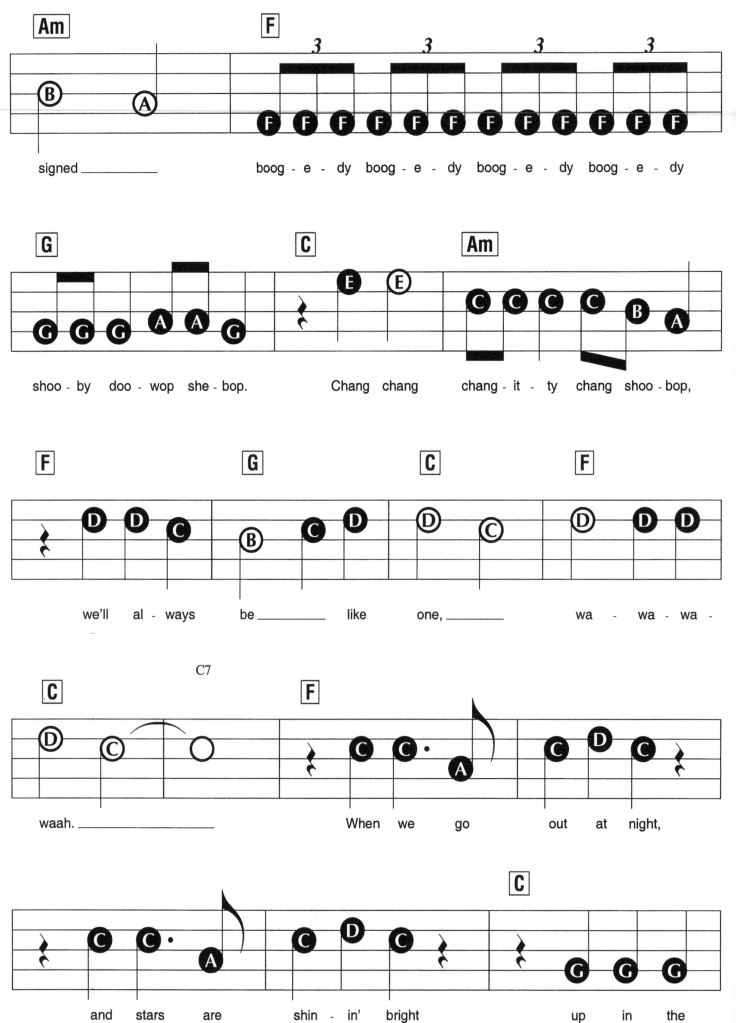

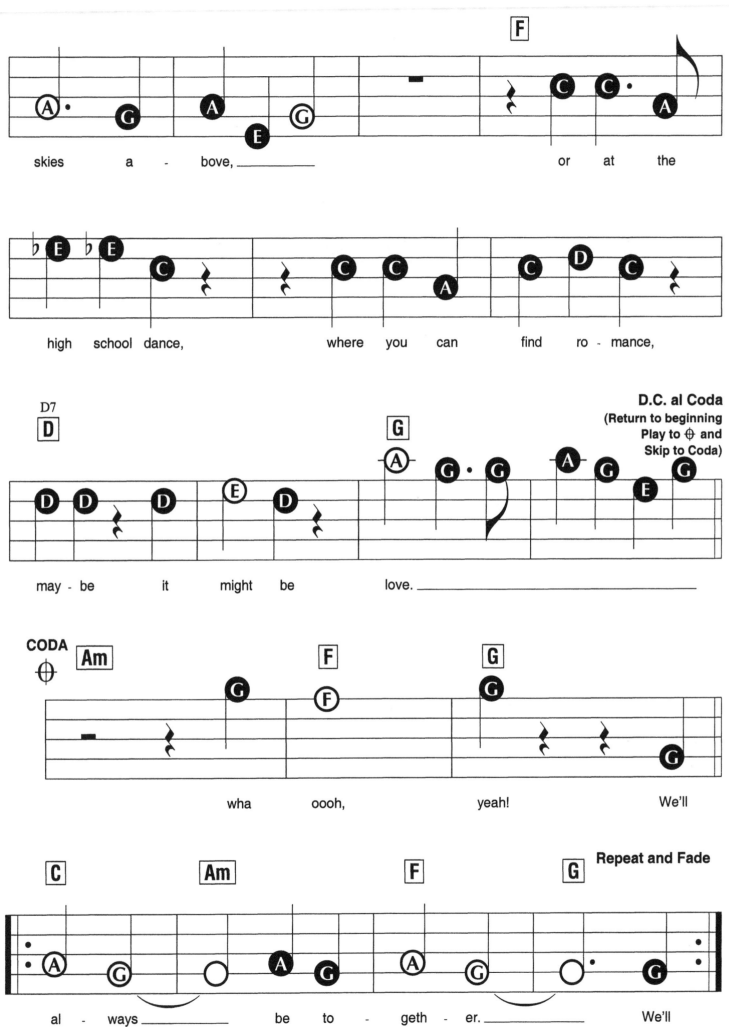

Look at Me, I'm Sandra Dee
(Reprise)

Registration 10
Rhythm: Waltz

Lyric and Music by Warren Casey
and Jim Jacobs

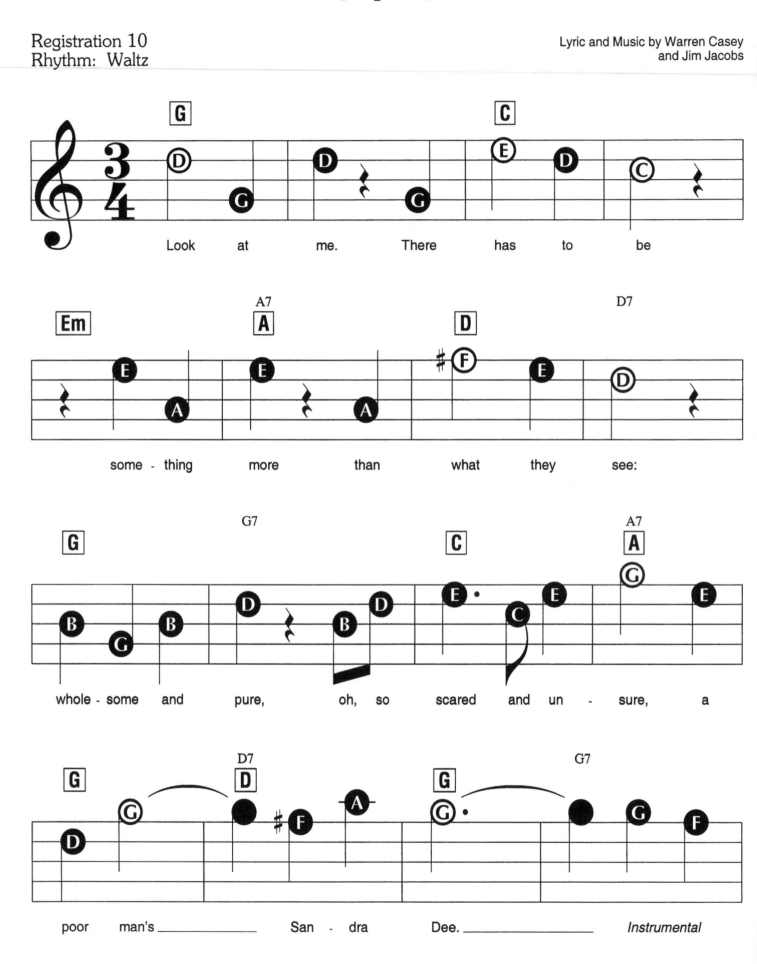

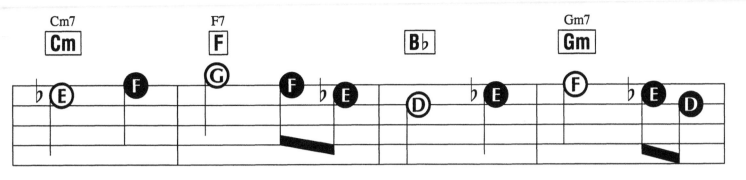

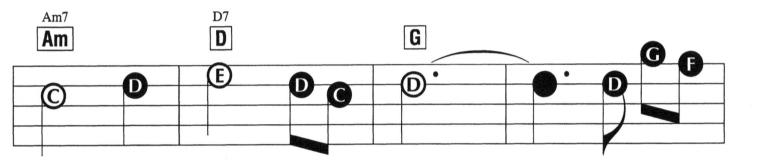

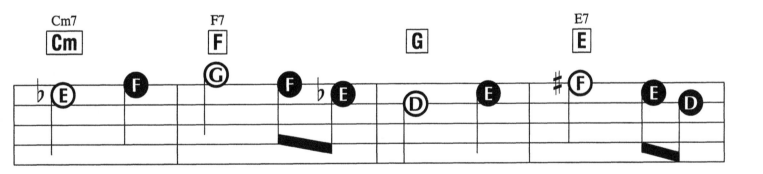

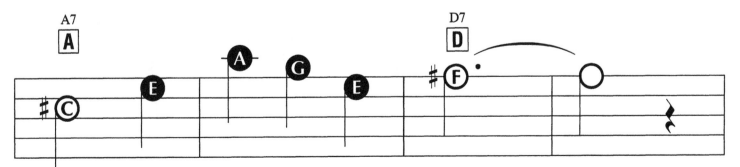

End instrumental

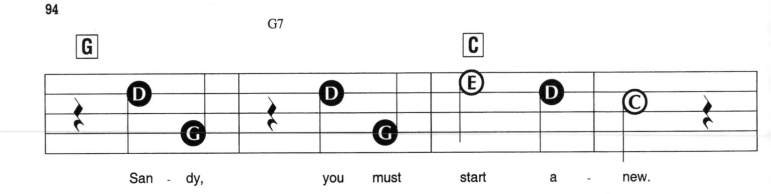

San - dy, you must start a - new.

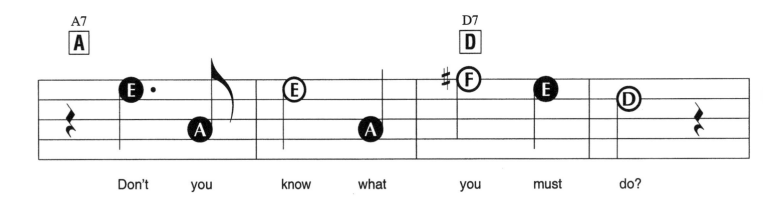

Don't you know what you must do?

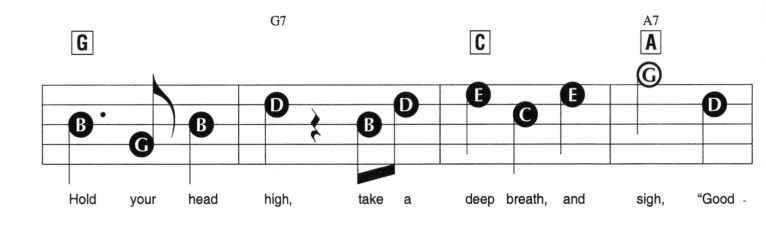

Hold your head high, take a deep breath, and sigh, "Good -

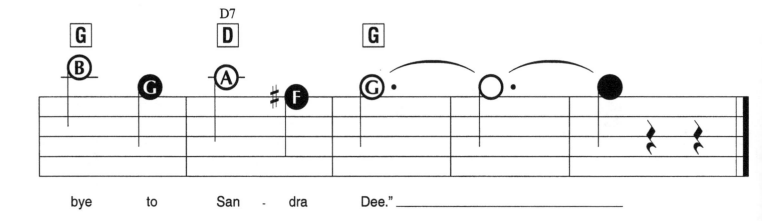

bye to San - dra Dee." _____

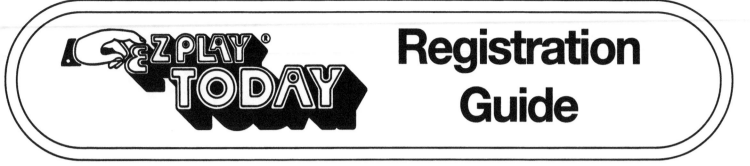

Registration Guide

- Match the Registration number on the song to the corresponding numbered category below. Select and activate an instrumental sound available on your instrument.

- Choose an automatic rhythm appropriate to the mood and style of the song. (Consult your Owner's Guide for proper operation of automatic rhythm features.)

- Adjust the tempo and volume controls to comfortable settings.

Registration

1	Flute, Pan Flute, Jazz Flute
2	Clarinet, Organ
3	Violin, Strings
4	Brass, Trumpet
5	Synth Ensemble, Accordion, Brass
6	Pipe Organ, Harpsichord
7	Jazz Organ, Vibraphone, Vibes, Electric Piano, Jazz Guitar
8	Piano, Electric Piano
9	Trumpet, Trombone, Clarinet, Saxophone, Oboe
10	Violin, Cello, Strings